Ending the Between Sales and Customers
Energy Professionals Edition

Jim Mathers and Andrey Sizov
with Nick Terrenzi

Copyright 2020 - Admiral Press

Admiral Press

1315 Cleveland Street Clearwater, FL 33755

© 2015-2020 Jim Mathers and Andrey Sizov. All Rights Reserved.

No part of this publication may be reproduced, stored in a retrieval system, or transmitted, in any form or by any means, without the prior permission in writing of either of the authors or their representative at Admiral Press, or as expressly permitted by law, or under terms agreed with the appropriate reprographics organization. Enquiries concerning reproduction outside the scope of the above should be sent to the Rights Department, Admiral Press, at the address above.

You must not circulate this book in any other binding or cover and you must impose the same condition on any acquirer.

Library of Congress Control #2015942537

ISBN: 9798635674789

Notes from readers of the first edition:

I've read the book twice. The 1st time a few days after you sent it to me and again over the weekend. I want my kids to read it since the advice is as much about life itself as it is about sales! There were quite a few chapters about goals and being honest with yourself that I've been harping on with my children since they were small – mainly due to the hard lessons their dad learned.

From a personal sales career perspective, Advice 8 – "fighting with customers," Advice 17 – about "perfect" being the enemy of "good," and Advice 14 and 39 – about speaking in the customer's language and not creating confusion, all resonated with me. Advice 40 – the 100% coefficient of efficiency will bring a smile to anyone who takes sales seriously. From an overall career perspective, I appreciated Advice 30 – Fundamentals of Success. Any reference to Mark Twain is a plus in my mind.

My biggest take away was in Advice 44 – "sales is the service provided to help the customer make the best choice" – a novel way of looking at the career.

Thank you for sending this to me.

Best of luck,

John Belgiovine,
Director of Sales Direct Energy

I absolutely loved this book! It has given me a whole new viewpoint on what "sales" really is! I am a single mom, I own my own business and I used to feel uncomfortable with the word "sales." I really didn't like to "sell" my customers.

The way Jim talks about the Cold War between customers and salesmen clarified for me why "sales" became a bad word. Now I know how to make "selling" an enjoyable experience for me, and my customers.

I give as much beneficial information as possible to my clients and the more I do, the more they buy from me and the happier they are.

I really feel like a champion now as I've made more sales than ever before in my life and this has resulted in more happy clients. In just 6 months I have 10x'd my sales. This is the best sales book I've ever read! Thank you!!!!

Josi Valerio
Entrepreneur

"Very concise and practical information that I can apply to my daily life. It was easy to understand, and I liked it so much that I read the whole book in two sittings. I see where I failed in the sales games in the past while reading this. Thanks Jim and please write more books in the future."

D.A.

"This is the best book on sales and the life attitudes necessary for sales with happiness that I have ever read or heard of. No one could miss being a super-salesman if the data in this book were truly applied, and diligently persisted."

B.N.

"One of the best books on sales. Breaking many stereotypes. Kind of actual attitude to the sales issue. It's giving you the 100% working technology for closing the deals being really helpful to your costumers and without using any manipulation. And is able to change your life cause you're using sales everyday selling your ideas at work even to your parents, kids and spouse or whoever."

K.F.

"Wow what a story that goes with this book. Aptly named. You got to get it to get the story. I am and have been a professional sales trainer myself and have read MANY books on the subject, however this one is highly unusual. It does not beat one up all about how you got to push, push, push to sell. Rather these guys take the path of interest. The interest that a salesperson needs to have in his potential customers in order to service his customers with utmost sincerity.

These two have been obviously been around the block and, using their techniques, a salesperson can not only sleep at night, he or she can be PROUD to be a part of the industry which brings to the public that which they need, smoothly and with integrity.

I am ordering several more copies for my whole Sales Team.

Thanks Jim and Andrey, you knocked it out of the park!"

D.O.

"This book contains some of the most accurate, useful and practical fundamentals of any I have ever seen on the topic of sales. Also, it is written in a simple, easy-to- follow style with no long paragraphs and no chapters that go on forever. Jim Mathers does an outstanding job of going straight to what is important, without wasting time with a whole bunch of "filler" data that you can't actually use. Very few things in this world happen without professional sales people somewhere on the line. This book will be a great help to them and to any company that employs them."

L.A.

DEDICATION

This book is dedicated to salesmen of every sex, race, religion and political ideology on this planet.

Salesmen are a vital necessity to every booming economy on Earth.

Nearly 8 billion people have something in common: They buy or trade some commodity – water, food, beans, coffee, salt, computers, phones, etc. - every single day of the year.

For ease of communication and rapid dissemination of basic concepts, we use the terms "he" and "salesman" in this book to refer to any woman or man who sells any type of commodity or service.

We are less concerned with being politically correct, and more concerned with creating EFFECTIVE & WEALTHY sales professionals!

Thank you,

Jim & Andrey

INDEX

PART 1: MINDSET	27
Advice #1 The Champion's Definition of "Sales"	28
Advice #2 Believe, and You Will See	30
Advice #3 Be Yourself and Don't Pretend	33
Advice #4 What You Should Do If You Want More	36
Advice #5 Fight Towards Your Goal	39
Advice #6 Don't Fall into the Opinion Trap	42
Advice #7 Don't Fall into the "Prove Yourself" Trap	45
Advice #8 Err on the Side of More Action	50
Advice #9 Keep Yourself Alive	53
Advice #10 Avoid the "Hard" Work Trap: Follow Your Passion	56
Advice #11 What You Actually Offer the Customer	60
Advice #12 Never be Afraid to Lose a Customer	63
Advice #13 Never Forget You're the Swan, Not the Ugly Duckling	66
Advice #14 How to Be a Wealthy Sales Champion	69
PART 2: PROSPECTING	71
Advice #15 Be Friendly and Engaging with People You Meet	72
Advice #16 Overcome Scarcity	77
Advice #17 Broaden Your Point of View Regarding Prospects	80
PART 3: RESEARCH	82
Advice #18 Be Prepared	83
Advice #19 Look at Your Presentation Through the Eyes of the Customer	85
PART 4: CONTACT	87
Advice #20 Winners Take Action	88
Advice #21 Don't Be Stopped by Failure or "Fear"	

of Failure 91
Advice #22 Daily Drilling for Success 94
Advice #23 Having Real Conversations 96

PART 5: INTERVIEW 100
Advice #24 Understand the Customer's Viewpoint on Quality 101
Advice #25 Be the Financial Advisor 103
Advice #26 Listen! 105
Advice #27 Set the Next Meeting 107
Advice #28 When Selling: Act Like You 109
Advice #29 Love What You Are Doing 113
Advice #30 Ask the Customer for Benefits 115

PART 6: QUALIFY 117
Advice #31 Honor and Respect Your Customer 118
Advice #32 Always, Always Comfortably Persist 121
Advice #33 Helping the Customer Choose the Best Option 123

PART 7: EDUCATION
Advice #34 Excel in Value 126
Advice #35 Remember What Motivates People 129
Advice #36 Watch Your Language 131
Advice #37 Build and Maintain a Strong Position with Your Customers 134
Advice #38 Why Salespeople Stop Liking their Products 136
Advice #39 Love What You Have, and Be Willing to Share with Others 139
Advice #40 Before You Take, You Must Give 141
Advice #41 Practice the Two Main Qualities 143
Advice #42 Don't Drive the Customer Away 145
Advice #43 Help the Customer Make the Best Choice 149
Advice #44 The Four Things You *Should* Talk About 150

Advice #45 Always Think of the Future	152
Advice #46 Getting Customers to Fully Understand Value	154
Advice #47 Fall in Love with Your Product	157
PART 8: AGREEMENT	**160**
Advice #48 Don't Create a "Battle" Scenario	161
Advice #49 Learn Why People Really Buy	163
Advice #50 Raise Your Sales Efficiency	166
Advice #51 Don't Just Talk About Advantages — Demonstrate Them	169
Advice #52 Never Sell Second-Rate	172
Advice #53 Appreciate What the Customer Gives to You	175
Advice #54 Learn Not to Make These 2 Fatal Mistakes	177
Advice #55 Don't Prevent Your Own Sales	179
PART 9: THE CLOSE	**182**
Advice #56 Don't Have a Scarcity Mindset	183
Advice #57 Use "I'll Think About It" to Continue the Conversation	186
Advice #58 Always Create Word of Mouth	190
Advice #59 Overcoming Your Worst Enemy: Doubt	193
Advice #60 Learn from Your Mistakes and Move On — Mistakes Are Not Failures	197
Rules, Laws & Principles	202
Sales Code of Honor	207
Photos	216

Introduction

The Cold War, a period of high tension between the two biggest nuclear powers on the planet, Russia and the United States, peaked in 1985. The fear of nuclear annihilation grew continuously after WWII and held the attention of every major world power. When the Berlin Wall was knocked down in 1989, marking the end of the Cold War, the whole world breathed a sigh of relief.

Nuclear war was a "war" that neither side could ever really win. The one point all nations agreed upon was that all-out nuclear war would affect every other country and living thing on the planet.

The main problem of the Cold War was the constant uncertainty and distrust on both sides of the negotiating table. During the summer and fall of 1985, Russian Navy anti-submarine corvette officer Lt. Andrey Sizov and United States Navy submarine officer Lt. Jim Mathers were involved in Cold War operations in the North Atlantic that involved searching for and potentially being ordered to destroy each other.

Today, these two former Cold War enemies have joined together in peace and understanding to solve a different kind of war — a war that has been going on for centuries: **the war between sales and customers.**

It happens every day in every marketplace in the world. Customers have been pitched to, run over, worn down, "sold," harassed, lied to, sucked up to, "taken care of" or bribed for centuries. Likewise, salespeople have been lied to, "sold," harassed, bribed, knocked down, put down, abandoned, demoralized and left in the dust. Talk to the average salesperson and they will tell you, "It's a war out there." Ask the average customer and they will say, "You just can't trust a salesperson."

It's an accepted rule that 20 percent of the salespeople make 80 percent of the sales. What are those successful salespeople doing right? Why are most salespeople fighting all day every day just to make a living? Why is the sales process a fight in the first place for most salespeople? Why do customers feel like they need a defense? Why is it a battle? Who is winning? Are we doomed to a never-ending war?

The observations of two lifetimes are gathered in this book — regarding the winning attitudes of champion sales professionals (simply referred to as "Champions") and handling customers correctly with the goal of *ending* the war between customers and sales professionals.

Russian business coach and author Andrey Sizov and American business owner and sales trainer Jim Mathers disclose principles that have proven to be the foundation of Champions. Andrey and Jim share the same basic philosophy regarding successful actions of Champions. They were former enemies, worlds apart, speaking different languages, but both had developed the exact same concept of how to train the very best salespeople. They have been teaching salespeople how to be professionals and gain the wealth they deserved by being the best in their profession for over 30 years on two different continents.

Outlined here are 60 simple and easy to understand lessons — called "Advices" — useful for any consultant, sales professional, sales manager or sales executive; no matter how much or how little experience they have in the field of professional sales.

Whether you are doing phone sales, door-to-door sales,

retail store sales, or large commercial enterprise sales, the basic fundamentals that lead to increasing wealth and success are the same, no matter what language you speak or what country you live in.

These lessons are also extremely useful for entrepreneurs, small business owners and managers, multi-level marketers, artists and anyone who has a product or service they would like to get other people to buy.

There *is* a correct way to sell to people that leads to high customer satisfaction, high commissions and high repeat and referral sales.
Study these fundamental rules and laws, practice them every day, and if you master these, you will become a true Champion and earn the wealth you deserve.

Let's make a deal:

We'll tell you what we've learned over the past 30 years.

Then you observe what is useful and interesting for you.

And you decide which lessons you choose to use.

Agreed?

Good! Let's get started!

Andrey

Note:

For your convenience and quick reference later, the primary principles used in the advices are listed out at the end of this book, referencing the advices from which they came.

Introduction to the *Energy Professionals Edition*

One factor that differentiates professional consultants from retail sales professionals is that the ultimate goal is a long-term relationship of providing our commercial and industrial customers multiple solutions that make their activities more efficient, more effective at delivering their products, and some would say most importantly, to increase their overall profitability. That would be true for most professional consultants in any type of industry.

I want to let you know that the lessons that we have learned over the past few decades of sales experience apply to any type of sales or consulting professional. But, in this edition, I want to add specific energy consulting & sales experiences from my past two decades of energy consulting experience to our original advices.

Andrey and I have tried to highlight the best characteristics of a champion sales professional who really cares about the client in front of them and who finds out exactly what service or product each client really needs to improve their overall profitability.

The way this book is structured, and the tools contained herein, will empower anyone from any background who is interested in increasing their personal earning power as a consultant or sales professional. Our goal is and has always been to help our friends to be better versions of themselves and to be able to create lifelong relationships, providing true and honest value to their customers, clients, colleagues and co-workers.

Every great organization or sales team normally has a team meeting on a regular basis and has each person name out their specific customer line-ups and sales goals for the upcoming day, week, month or quarter. In addition to helping you personally, this book can be used as a tool to "sharpen the axe" of your sales teams on a regular basis. It can also help as a tool for managers to increase sales and productivity across the boards.

I'm excited for you to be able to take these advices and tools and utilize them in expanding your business. I know that it will make for a much more natural sales process, and I believe that anyone who uses this book will be able to increase and improve their sales and be able to build a prosperous business within any industry.

Intended Audience

This special *Energy Professionals Edition* of *Ending the War Between Sales and Customers* has been created with the intention of helping energy industry professionals expand their customer base, and to help them take their businesses to the next level. In building a successful sales and consulting business there are three particular areas that define its growth:

1. The first and most obvious area — and the core subject of this book — is the subject of sales and conducting sales the most effective way within the energy industry. This book is for the salesperson looking to increase their ability to successfully attract, close and service their customers.

2. The second area that we've touched upon in this book is the subject of recruitment and attracting new agents. In building an expanding consulting business, you want to make sure that you're always recruiting professionals that are consistent with your values and company culture. Recruitment plays a strong role in

the expansion of an agency, so this book is also for any professional recruiter seeking the right people and wishing to relate to recruitment prospects in a deeper way.

3. The third component is leadership development. So equally this book is for business owners and executives in the process of explosive business expansion and seeking to empower their sales leaders to be able to drive that expansion and create new leaders.

Energy Professionals Perspective

Within many of the advices, you'll see an **Energy Professionals Perspective**. I added these to this special edition to focus the scope of advices specifically for energy consultants. I hope you find them helpful.

An intended "side-effect" of this particular edition is that it also educates corporate purchasers, Controllers and CFOs on how exactly they should be treated by any sales or consulting professional throughout the purchasing process.

Action Items and Journal

As you proceed through the advices, you'll see that there are *Action Items* following many of them.

You should keep a journal of your progress through the advices, and of your exercises with the Action Items. By doing so, you can monitor your progress in learning these skills and — more importantly — how you utilize them in your daily business in making presentations and interacting with your clients. The blank pages are there for you to record your thoughts, questions, observations and realizations.

On that note, I am always happy to receive your feedback on your successes along the way. You can email me directly any time!

Jim@KnowledgeIsPower.today

Here's to YOU achieving your wildest dreams!

Jim

About the Sales Process Used in This Edition
by Nick Terrenzi

An incredibly well-researched sales process has been utilized in this Energy Professionals Edition of *Ending the War Between Sales and Customers*. This process was developed after numerous years of experience between myself and my wife, Lisa; between the two of us, we worked with a great many Fortune 100 and Fortune 500 companies — and my wife was the CEO of an Inc. 500 company as well. When it came right down to it, all of these companies had the same problem: sales.

The 80/20 Rule

There's a rule or law, also known as the Pareto Principle, that states that 80 percent of effects come from 20 percent of the causes. In sales, this rule is modified to state that 80 percent of the sales are made by 20 percent of salespeople, which has been observed and written about since the 1940s.

We encountered this problem again, and again, and again. We're great at sales training and we could walk into just about any company and make the sales go up. But they weren't able to maintain it after we were gone.

We realized that, in order to handle that problem, we needed to fully address the situation.

The Percentages

We obviously knew that if we could improve those top 20 percent, we could improve sales in a company. But what if someone wasn't in that 20 percent? If they were inconsistent, they were just labeled as such. There was no solution. Nobody was asking, "Wait a minute — how do you fix *them*?"

The Realization at Microsoft

Our discoveries originally came about when Lisa and I were doing a project with Microsoft. Microsoft was encountering challenges with its partner network. Each Microsoft partner was an independently owned business, so Microsoft didn't have a direct management line into partners — yet they needed those partners to sell.

The 80/20 rule was very apparent in this situation. Even within the Microsoft partner network, 80 percent of the sales were being made by 20 percent of the partners. Then if you went in and spoke to the partner companies, you found it there also: 80 percent of the sales were being made by 20 percent of the sales reps.

As we continued our research, we found that this issue was not exclusive to Microsoft by any stretch. We found it everywhere around the world.

Over-Focus on Closing

When we began really digging into the problems to resolve them, we realized that despite billions of dollars being spent yearly on sales training, that 80/20 rule persisted — going all the way back to the 1940s when it was observed. It had *never* been improved.

One of the most major discoveries we made was that most sales training focuses almost exclusively on closing. Of course! Closing is important — that's where the money is made. But there's a great deal more to a sales process than closing.

You'll see this virtually anywhere. You can go into a mall and just start walking into stores and meeting salespeople. You'll find that every conversation begins with a push toward the close. Even a "Can I help you?" is an assumption that you need help, rather than just a simple welcome to the store.

When it came down to it, this was the number one reason that salespeople have had so much trouble — and such bad reputations — down through the years. This is why they create such incredible resistance: from the very beginning of the conversation, they're trying to *close the prospect*.

Most salespeople avoid most or all of the steps and skip right to the close. If you want a live demonstration of how futile that is, just walk up to someone and try and close them. You can feel that resistance.

The Common Factors in Sales Success

On further research, we discovered that there are 8 factors that all successful salespeople — yes, that top 20 percent — have in common. In our company 80/20 Sales Technology, we have isolated these factors and call them the 8 Cs of Selling:

Communication — Obviously you must have great communication skills to sell.
Control — A salesperson must have an ability to control. As a prospect or customer, we all want to be positively controlled or guided through the sales process by someone with great communication skills.
Contact — The ability to generate rapport and make that initial contact is vital, for it is here you start to build trust.

Confidence — A salesperson must obviously come across as totally confident in what they're doing.
Competence — As a consumer or buyer, you always want to go to an expert. You can spot this person — they totally know their business. And they use the same product they're selling.
Certainty — The last thing you want, either as a business owner or a prospect, is a salesperson who is uncertain. Much of this has to do with product knowledge, but it's actually an understanding of much more than product knowledge. It is also knowledge of the technology behind what they're selling, and the services. On top of that, you really want a salesperson who is certain of *how to sell*.
Closing — Of course there's a whole skillset to closing.
Customer Relationship — This is a factor largely missing from sales today — they forget that sales, especially in the energy industry, is a lifelong relationship. A relationship must be maintained.

The advices in this book will help anyone develop and improve the 8 factors common to the champion sales professionals of the world.

Sales Process

The 8 Cs above are what we utilize to bring a prospect smoothly through the sales process, which we are going to cover now.

The advices in this book are laid out under each of the sales process steps to which they correspond. You will therefore discover a great deal more about each sales process step as you go through the book. Below I have provided some basic information about each sales process step.

As a note before I lay out the sales process: this is a pretty simple process. As in all things in life, simple is always better. You'll note that you may have more detail in your particular sales process, which is fine — but you'll find that this process will encompass any sales process out there in the world today, no matter what language you speak.

I'm going to work the sales process backwards, as that's how it was researched — it was literally "reverse engineered" back from the close.

7. Closing
At the end comes closing. It's the last step of the process. Ask for the signature.

6. Agreement
Just before closing is the Agreement step. The salesperson has brought you all the way through the process, you've actually or virtually shaken hands and you've decided to purchase. There's a small step in between Agreement and Close where you handle paperwork, logistics and anything else you need to wrap up — and that takes you from Agreement to Close.

5. Education
Just prior to Agreement is the Education step. Education is incredibly important, especially in the energy industry. In this industry we're educating CFOs, COOs, CEOs, operations professionals, maintenance professionals, business owners & general managers, helping create a more energy efficient building, improving the building air quality, reducing overall costs while increasing profit and helping companies set a strategy to achieve their sustainability goals — and prospects and clients need to be educated on all of these things.

But it doesn't actually matter what your product or service is. Your task as a sales consultant is to educate that prospect.

The end result of education is an inspired prospect. They're inspired to take action. When you've educated someone and properly inspired them, how do you think you'll do in closing the sale? Answer: brilliantly.

In addition to skipping straight to the Close, you'll also find a lot of salespeople skip right to this Education step without going through any of the prior steps to Education. We've all experienced this. You'll find you're immediately bored because, prior to launching into this verbose explanation of their product or service, the salesperson hasn't discovered anything about you: your needs, wants, desires or problems. There's no alignment of this Education to something you might actually be interested in.

In either scenario — skipping to Education or skipping to the Close — you'll never inspire anyone into action, so you'll never get to Agreement, and then to the actual Close. This is why *80 percent* of salespeople fail to close.

4. Qualifying
Prior to Education is Qualifying. Here, you're finding out why the prospect should purchase your product or service — from their point of view. You're finding out what problems they have. What are they running into? What are their goals? What is their previous experience?

The trap that a salesperson can fall into is that they've been through the interview process so many times that they just go into a meeting assuming they "know already." This completely robs a prospect of their own conviction and determination — and you won't make a sale by doing that.

In the Qualifying step, you'll find that you'll need to utilize some education just to get the qualifying steps done. But mainly you're just trying to find out all about the prospect in relation to your offering.

3. Contact and Interview
But you won't make it through the Qualifying step if you haven't done the two prior steps, Contact and Interview, correctly and completely. That's because, in order to get a prospect to tell you about their lives, their hopes, their dreams, their problems, they need to trust you enough to tell you what they're really thinking.

It is during these stages that you create trust with the prospect. The acid test of trust is simply this: did the prospect call you back or respond to your email? I can always tell when these steps have been skipped or skimped on, because there's the evidence, every time: no call back, or no further response to your communication.

2. Research
There is a step prior to making the initial contact, and that is Research. A massive mistake salespeople make is not researching their prospect. Do your homework! Really understand that prospect before you meet them. Do they know the same people you know? Today with social media, this step is much easier than it was years back. For example, you can discover you have a friend in common; call that friend and gain an introduction.

1. Prospecting
Prospecting, as you'll discover under this step in the book, is a matter of really knowing your product or service, what makes you different (your Unique Selling Proposition) and having a fast, powerful "elevator pitch" to quickly give

someone. The key to prospecting is a total confidence in introducing many people to what you do.

In Sequence
Now let's look at this in sequence:

1. You **Prospect** by confidently telling as many people as possible about your product or service.
2. You conduct your **Research,** so you have an idea of who you're going to be talking to.
3. In **Contact and Interview**, you're developing enough trust so that the prospect will tell you what they're thinking.
4. Then you can ask the **Qualifying** questions and actually obtain honest answers.
5. Now you go into **Education**, and they're inspired to take action. Because you've actually gotten to know them, Education is precise for that prospect. Are they going to be interested? You bet!
6. You're easily going to get them into **Agreement**,
7. And then transition right to the **Close**.

And always remember: the only way a sale will close is if all the earlier steps were completed.

Good luck, and good selling!

Nick

Part 1: The Champion's Mindset

> "You were born to win, but to be a winner, you must plan to win, prepare to win, and expect to win."
> Zig Ziglar

Advice #1
The Champion's Definition of "Sales"

Here is the definition of "sales" that Champions use:

Sales is the service of helping a client choose the best *product or service.*

True sales success is defined as helping so many people make the best choices that the number of customers who buy is more than anyone else expects to be humanly possible. This may be the most important chapter in this book. It's too simple to be believed, but it's the most fundamental idea that true professionals apply successfully every single day.

— — — — — — — — — — — — — — — — — —

Energy Professionals Perspective

As I increased my understanding of the electric and gas utility industry, I increased my competence and my ability to communicate easily about our products and services. I continue to make sure all of our energy advisors are learning more every day. When we are able to fully educate our clients on how they can save money and be more energy efficient, they really appreciate our help and they understand their problems and even more importantly, they understand the solutions we offer to handle their energy related issues.

Having a clear understanding of your own products and services allows you to really help your client understand what their needs are, and they have confidence that you can help them choose the best product or service.

"Knowledge relaxes me. Football is about playing faster. You play faster when you know more."
— *Marshall Faulk*

Action Items

1. Write down what the word "sales" means to you in your own words.
2. Now think of 5 different sales situations you have witnessed that do *not* fit this definition. Examples: Close the person no matter what they need or want. Manipulate people to say yes even if the product is not right for them. Upsell people as much as you can get away with before the customer realizes what's happening.
3. Now think of 5 sales situations you have witnessed that *do* fit the definition above.
4. Write down how this viewpoint of sales can create long term successful relationships with your clients.

Advice #2
Believe, and You Will See

Let's get right to the core of the matter.

Love, duty, honor, courage, beauty, harmony — these qualities *do* exist in life.

If it were not true, life would be a sad and dreary prospect. Those who want to see these qualities, *do see them*, whenever and wherever they look. These qualities exist, whether you believe in them or not.

The following principle works here: *"Believe, and you will see."*

If you *believe* these good qualities of life do exist, you will *see evidence* of them around you. You will use them to provide benefits to others as well as yourself. If you *don't* believe in them, you won't see them, and then they won't exist in your life. If you believe that people are only out for themselves, that it's a "dog eat dog" world, then you won't see these ideals, and as a result, you won't attract these honorable qualities for the benefit of yourself and others.

Decide for yourself. It's your choice. You're at a crossroads and you can go in two different directions. Where do you want to go? Only you can decide for yourself. If you truly don't believe that love, honor, duty, faith, courage, beauty and harmony exist in this world, put this book down and walk away, because this book is based on that foundation.

We will tell you about the road that goes toward success and true wealth, which in fact is always with you; you shouldn't have to chase after money as the only goal and stress yourself out every day. Choose wisely.

The stars shine only for those who look up at the night sky.

Energy Professionals Perspective

As professional consultants and advisors to business leaders, we should strive to pursue higher laws such as the Golden Rule, and ascendant principles. By "ascendant principles" we mean those principles which apply to a higher law, beyond simply ourselves.

The higher laws require the belief and faith that when you perform good acts, good will come back to you. Faith is defined as "belief in things not seen." Faith requires us to act in a certain way, knowing that good things will occur as a result of our actions while not having any evidence that this is true. A consistent practice of treating others how you'd want to be treated is a must for any long-term, sustainable success.

For example, it could be said that there are two versions of the Golden Rule. The more basic form is, "You scratch my back and I'll scratch yours." The "higher law" or ascendant principle version would be, "Do unto others as you would have them do unto you."

Action Items

1. Think of 5 times you were treated the way you would want to be treated.
2. Now think of 5 times you treated someone else the way you would want to be treated.
3. Note any thoughts or realizations in your journal.
4. Feel free to email any successes to: Jim@KnowledgeisPower.today

Advice #3
Be Yourself and Don't Pretend

You are very able, and as a result of your native ability, you have a huge potential of success. In fact, you were born wealthy and successful! *This is your natural condition.*

Maybe you have been taught that you are not wealthy or successful and you feel you have to "pretend" to be something you're not, in order to be successful and rich. This pretense causes stress and tension.

Be who you actually are!

If you don't have everything working perfectly yet, just admit to yourself: "It's not perfect yet." As long as you continue to practice and learn to be a true professional, you will start to be perfect more often. "Be yourself" wholeheartedly without trying to be more or less than you are. Don't pretend to be something you are not.

Some people, misunderstanding this law, try to create a false picture of success. This causes a lot of stress. They try to "appear" happy and wealthy and even try harder to "believe" it. They work hard to convince others and spend a lot of their attention and time in this effort. They act nice and kind to a customer only because they want the customer's money, not because they want to help the customer.

This false pretense really becomes obvious when the customer suddenly decides that they are not going to buy. The salesperson sees the sale is lost and thinks, "That's it, there's no more reason to pretend to be a polite person; now I can be myself." At that moment, the customer will notice a change in the salesperson's attitude and will hear fewer flattering remarks from the salesperson who is no longer pretending to be polite.

Stress and tension occur because of the desire to show others an attitude that actually doesn't exist inside. This causes strong turmoil and discomfort inside the salesperson. Over time, they will stop selling as much as they were before, or just quit that job. They will create different reasons to "explain" why they quit selling: "The company is bad," "The sales manager is bad," "The commission plan is unfair," and so on.

The idea is simple: *To have more success and money in sales, be who you really are and stop working under so much stress and strain.*

This works in any area of life, not just sales.

— — — — — — — — — — — — — — — — — — —

Energy Professionals Perspective

There is a fine line between "fake it till you make it" and selling the vision of a greater tomorrow.

If you plan to be successful, don't ever be fooled into thinking you have to be somebody other than who you actually are. In fact, the more genuine you are with people, the more success you'll end up having.

Having confidence begins with seeing your future and knowing you can create it.

Many of the best advisors starting in the energy industry could afford nice cars and expensive toys to impress their friends and prospects, instead, they successfully made millions helping many customers before deciding to upgrade their cars and material possessions. The car and the clothes do not make the person — it's quite the opposite.

The key is to be happy with what you have right now and build a solid foundation of excellent service before buying the expensive toys.

I have a very good friend who bought his first jet a few years ago. I heard comments that he was just showing off. He spent over 25 years training sales professionals and building a solid foundation of wealth before buying that jet with cash. He did not borrow money to buy a jet to show off to people so he could sell them something. He never pretended to be something he wasn't. He wasn't trying to impress people, instead he focused on helping many other people succeed.

Set a good example for your people.

Action Items

1. In your journal, write down 5 traits about yourself — strengths that you feel you can bring to a client relationship — that are more consistent with being yourself.
2. Think of 5 people you met who you knew were pretending to be something they were not.
3. Think of 5 people you have met or know about that truly are exactly who they say they are.
4. Write down your 1-year goals, 3-year goals, 5-year goals and 10-year goals.

Advice #4
What You Should Do If You Want More

Realize that if you want to have more (sales, money, time, etc.) than you have right now, you should do something *different* from what you are currently doing. Your daily actions need to change. You need to consistently do these new actions if you want more success. This, as a rule, is something unusual, and is connected with breaking out of your current "comfort zone." It will take your decision to change! It will take consistent effort and practice!

Any new and better goal is *always* located *outside* your comfort zone. *Always!*

To achieve any new goal requires persistent effort; if it were easy, you would see everyone around you achieving new goals every day. So, in order to really break out of your current comfort zone, you need to be willing to work harder than everyone else in order to live a more happy and wealthy life than before. This is not as difficult as it may seem at first.

Everything new and worthwhile seems difficult... until it becomes easy as you learn the secret of how to do it.

You have to ask yourself: *Do you really want to be a rich and successful sales professional?*

Be honest with yourself.

Be willing to change your mind.

Decide! Then go into action!

It is a lot more fun being able to buy your friends dinner

without having to worry about paying for rent.

Energy Professionals Perspective

Do simple daily consistent successful actions.

When I first decided I was going to start an energy consulting business, I realized I would need to be more disciplined in my daily activities. I needed to change my thought process and actually do simple successful actions every single day, without getting bored or frustrated or upset that the success did not come immediately.

Every night I would review my goals. I had a simple but effective plan of actions that I performed every day. I started this business nowhere near any comfort zone. Some days I was terrified I would fail, that I would not be able to sign up my first big client. But every day I did the same actions over and over. Simple actions. I had my list of potential clients. I emailed them, faxed them, called them every day. I made appointments for prospects and I always kept those appointments, even when several prospects blew me off. I was relentless in getting that first contract signed. I did it. It took me three months to get the first three contracts signed. Two of the three clients didn't pay our invoices. One client did. That was enough to launch a 20-year career as a professional energy sales consultant. My faith in my successful actions paid off.

Action Items: Going Outside Your Comfort Zone

1. In your journal, write down 5 activities — even small ones will do — that are outside your comfort zone.
2. Go and do them. Remember the first 10 seconds of any action outside your comfort zone are the hardest. Just force yourself to take that first step, say the first word, start!
3. Repeat this exercise until you feel confident that you can step outside your comfort zone, even to some small degree.
4. Note the results in your journal.

Action Items: Pre-Planning Your Day

1. Before going to sleep, write down 5 action items that you need to do to move your business forward, and 5 prospects you're going to call tomorrow.
2. As you go to sleep, visualize and create in your mind a positive outcome of each action item or meeting.
3. Upon waking, review your 5 action items, and 5 prospects you're going to call. Note how you feel. Do you feel more positive about approaching those people? Have you visualized the successful outcome for them?
4. Make these actions part of "Stepping Outside Your Comfort Zone" and take them today.
5. Track and note the results in your journal.

Advice #5
Fight Towards Your Goal

Champions win by constantly battling toward their goal, especially at the beginning stage. They never get upset if their first attempts are unsuccessful, and they achieve success because they don't quit moving toward their goal.

To win in life or sales, it's more important to keep moving forward toward your goal. Don't worry about making mistakes. True success lies in the willingness to keep trying, learning from your mistakes, and moving forward no matter how small some of the steps you take may be.

Keep moving forward! Don't quit! Don't fall back into the comfort zone of mediocrity.

If you are able to dream up a goal, you are able to achieve it.

There is no goal you can dream of that you can't achieve. But any dream will require you to *take consistent action* to bring it to reality. The size of your dream will determine how many actions you will have to take to achieve it. Every person can achieve their dream *if* they are willing to do all the actions necessary.

Are you willing to do what is necessary to achieve the goals you dream up?

The bigger your goals, the more actions you must be willing to take and continue as long as necessary to reach your goals and fulfill your dream.

You can achieve any goal that you can dream up, but only if you are willing to roll up your sleeves and persist in correct actions that move you closer and closer to your goal.

"Don't rest & don't stop — ever. Most valuable chips you have are your mind-set, actions, persistence & creativity."
— Grant Cardone

———————————————

Energy Professionals Perspective

Attitude, Activity and Attendance

I was taught you can really control three things in sales: your attitude, your activity (phone calls and emails) and your attendance.

Your attitude is 100% under your control at all times. Champions never blame other people for "ruining their attitude." No matter what happens, your attitude is based on your decision to be positive in the face of both good times and bad times. If a prospect suddenly changes their mind and does NOT sign your contract at the close, you don't throw things around the office or yell at your spouse. First of all, you should never hang your success on one prospect, ever! Second, if you have a good attitude, you will find out exactly what you did or didn't do to set up that close. This is totally your choice. You choose now to be in control of your attitude and your life or not.

Your activity level is again totally under your control. If you only make 10 phone calls a day to potential clients when the most successful people are making twice as many, that is your choice.

Attendance. Simple. Show up early for work every day. Be the last one to leave. Attend every single training event offered by your company. If no training is offered by your company, don't use that as an excuse. There are dozens of energy webinars given every week in our industry. Attend those trainings and watch your competence and confidence in your presentations continue to increase. Your prospects will appreciate it, and your peers will notice and hopefully follow your example. It's much more fun and rewarding to have an office full of champions than to have one great sales pro and a bunch of unhappy people in your office complaining about how bad the energy market is and how impossible it is to sell your service.

Discipline in these areas increases your chance to win big time!

Action Items

1. Write down a goal you really want to achieve — preferably one you want to achieve more than any other. This can be a goal of any size, short-term, mid-term or long-term.
2. Now write out a week's worth of actions that you can take, 1 each day, that move you forward toward your goal. Doesn't matter how small each action is — it moves you forward toward your goal.
3. Repeat this activity weekly, making the actions bigger and more encompassing as you go.
4. Keep track of the results in your journal.

Advice #6
Don't Fall into the Opinion Trap

People usually start off a new activity with desire and enthusiasm. But right at the outset, "opinions" start trapping them:

- *"Was it done with high quality and attention to detail?"*
- *"Was enough time spent preparing the product?"*
- *"Was enough training done first?"*

There seem to be many "expert" opinions on what is right and what is wrong. Some will advise you to not even start selling until your product or service or presentation is "perfect."

As a rule, those who *never* achieve success are so busy "perfecting" the product to the level of other's opinions that they never get out and talk to enough potential customers every single day.

Winners continually work to upgrade their knowledge, their skill and their product or service. *But* they never use that as a reason for not talking to more people than any of their competitors or co-workers.

This assumes you have a good, workable product or service that delivers what you promise. The emphasis is on *workable*!

When you start to do anything,
It's like you're writing on blank wall.
The tiniest mistake you make will stick out for all to see.
Those who do nothing, write nothing on the wall,
And they are always the worst critics of your "mistakes."
But the critic never gets anything done either.

So, beware the trap of another's "helpful" opinion.

Michael Jordan, one of the most successful basketball players of all-time, said:

"I've missed more than 9,000 shots in my career. I've lost almost 300 games. 26 times, I've been trusted to take the game winning shot and missed. I've failed over and over and over again in my life. And that is why I succeed."

Given his career, it's pretty obvious that Michael Jordan never stopped to listen to the "opinions" of others.

Energy Professionals Perspective

When you move into a new area of expertise such as energy, you can have a lot of self-doubt due to your lack of experience. Whether you have been in the general sales arena a couple years or a couple of decades, you have a lot of specific energy technology terms and services to learn before you can be a champion energy advisor.

If this is a new field for you to learn, you have to remember there are always going to be people around you who have failed in the past. They will *gladly* give you their opinions on why this job can't be done or how it's going to take you many years to make good money being an energy consultant.

Make sure that you don't fall victim to the opinions of other people on whether or not you're really going to be successful. Start with a *big* goal or a *big* dream of what you'd ultimately like to do and stay focused on moving toward that dream every day even though your execution may not be perfect in the beginning.

The opinion trap is dangerous especially when those opinions are negative. If you have people who are encouraging and positive, and their opinions are workable for successful action, then work with them. The only proof of this is your gradual success. You don't have to know every single detail of a full energy strategy before you start contacting prospects!

Action Items

1. Think of and write down 3 things that your product or service does to help your customer. Decide that you're really happy in helping others in that way.
2. Make a strong decision to increase the number of people that you're helping in those areas.
3. Write down your yearly, monthly & weekly goals.
4. Decide now that you will do whatever it honestly takes to achieve your goals.
5. Note the results in your journal.

Advice #7
Don't Fall Into the "Prove Yourself" Trap

The most dangerous trap is listening to everyone's opinions on quality and perfection and worrying about what someone else is going to say about your delivery or your product. This is especially difficult when there are many "clever" critics around. Their slogan is "Prove you're the best, then maybe I'll buy."

If you constantly try to prove yourself to others, you fall into a horrible trap. It will stop you and kill your dreams, unless you are fully aware of this trap.

If you focus all your efforts on avoiding failure and mistakes, or you fear looking like an idiot, you will lose. You may even forget your dreams and goals entirely and wander off looking for an "easier" job.

We're not just talking about the external critics (customers and co-workers and managers) we're also talking about *you* criticizing *you* (internal criticism). Sometimes you can be your own worst enemy.

This external and internal criticism can destroy your most important ability: the ability to take action and to take joy and pleasure in your own motion.

Fear of failure attracts failure like a magnet. Focus on the truth. The truth is, right at this moment, that you are able to take some action and get things done.

The more actions you take, the more good results you achieve. The more good results you achieve, the better and more professional you become. The more professional you are, the more successful you become.

- Winners are not born. They are made.
- Winners are not afraid to make mistakes.
- Winners are busy doing something effective, not sitting around and criticizing the efforts of others.

Jim's First Sales Experience

I was a professional nuclear engineer and I was ready for a new career and the opportunity to make a lot more money. My friend told me he made a ton of money every weekend. I believed him. I showed up at the meeting place for my first door-to-door sales experience, eager to learn and excited to meet the team.

I wore my nicest golf shorts and golf shirt. The training manager was late, so I had time to ask the dozen sales reps standing around about their experience with this awesome sales opportunity.

The first guy looked at me and said, "You can't sell in shorts, nobody will take you seriously!"

I was a little dismayed, but I reminded myself that my friend made a lot of money. I asked how many sales I could expect to make on my first day.

Everyone laughed and said, "Zero!"

At that moment the trainer walked in and started handing out area assignments. I was thinking I had made a big mistake and that I had just given up a beautiful golf day to waste my time. But as I was starting to slide out the door to escape, the trainer grabbed me and said, "Let's go!"

By this time my initial enthusiasm was dashed, but I had promised my friend I would try it out, and I really needed to increase my income.

The product was a discount card for a local car repair shop. It really was a no-brainer. The cost was $20, and the customer got 3 free oil changes worth $45, plus another $500 worth of discounts on car repairs. I was ready to buy one myself.

The trainer walked up to the first house, knocked on the door, explained the benefit of the discount card, collected the money and we walked away. It happened so fast; I wasn't even sure of what he had said to the customer.

After he sold five in a row, I told him to give me the discount card so I could sell the next customer. This was too easy! He was unbelievably comfortable talking to the customers, explaining the benefits, answering their questions, and collecting $20 bills. But he told me to wait, he had to show me how to handle an "objection."

The next guy was very serious and antagonistic. He wouldn't look or listen, no matter what the trainer said. After 10 minutes, the trainer gave up and we walked away.

I said, "You mean some people won't listen no matter what you say? Give me that discount card!"

I knocked on the next door and a 16-year-old boy answered. My first thought was to ask for his parents. My next thought was to practice my *first* pitch on this young guy. I decided to show him the card and explained the discounts and the other benefits.

He started laughing and pointed to his "new" car in the driveway (his "new" car was 20 years old.) He said he needed every service on the card and asked me to wait a minute while he grabbed some money. He came back with

$40 cash and said his best friend had a "new" car, too. I made a double commission on my very first sale.

I made mistakes that first day, but the trainer was there to help me out. I listened to his advice eagerly and made 20 sales that day — not zero! I earned $50 per hour, twice as much as I was making as a nuclear engineer.

I quit my government engineering job and I've been in sales ever since that day! And, I never stopped learning how to be more professional.

Important Rules I Learned My First Day of Selling:

- Sell something you like personally.
- Only take advice from successful, positive professionals.
- Ignore negative and critical people.
- Ignore your own fear and self-doubts and go into action.

"It is not the critic who counts; not the man who points out how the strong man stumbles, or where the doer of deeds could have done them better. The credit belongs to the man who is actually in the arena, whose face is marred by dust and sweat and blood; who strives valiantly; who errs, who comes short again and again, because there is no effort without error and shortcoming; but who does actually strive to do the deeds; who knows great enthusiasms, the great devotions; who spends himself in a worthy cause; who at the best knows in the end the triumph of high achievement, and who at the worst, if he fails, at least fails while daring greatly, so that his place shall never be with those cold and timid souls who neither know victory nor defeat."
— *Theodore Roosevelt*

Action Items

1. Think of 5 people who have been very supportive of you since you started your career.
2. Write down all the ways that they were supportive of you.
3. Send them a note just thanking them for their support and encouragement.
4. Note any thoughts or results in your journal.

Advice #8
Err on the Side of More Action

Here's another trap: you stop taking action because somebody else thinks that what you are doing or saying is wrong.

The result: *You stop and "think" instead of just going into action.*

How often does this occur in sales? Every day. For example:

- Sales reps won't approach those customers who don't look "friendly."
- Sales reps think it's "rude" to ask a lot of "personal" questions.
- It's not generally accepted to take an active interest in customers' problems.
- It's too hard to direct the customer's attention back to the benefits already discussed.
- If the customer says: "I need to think about it!" The sales rep thinks the sale is over (more on this in advices #23 and #57).

In each of these examples, sales reps stop to "think" about problems instead of going into action and just start communicating to the potential customer. They stop trying.

A Champion is willing and able to make any sales proposal, to anyone they choose. They don't stop to "think" any negative thoughts about anyone. They just go into action, confidently controlling their own attitude and communicating effectively with any customer.

Energy Professionals Perspective

Being in the energy industry, our livelihood is dependent upon the number of times we sit across from someone and present our products or services. However, sometimes we sit and reflect on failures that we've had, as opposed to finding ways we could improve and taking additional successful action.

One of the ways to solve this is, at the beginning of every week, try to book as many presentations into your week as you can, before you even get started on your week. And as you're going through your week's meetings and getting referrals, book as many appointments as far into the future as possible. This way, every day, you have no time to think about the failure or adversity that has happened to you in the past, because you're too busy doing the next presentation.

In a nutshell: you want to do *more* presentations to overcome past failure and adversity, not less.

"That some should be rich shows that others could become rich, and hence is just encouragement to industry and enterprise."
— *Abraham Lincoln*

Action Items

1. Take a good look at your last 30 days of activity.
2. Decide if this is in an unacceptable range, or an acceptable range. Would you rather keep it in the same range, or have more explosive growth?
3. Take a moment to describe the ideal amount of activity that you would like to have in a given week and month.
4. Sit down and work out how you're going to increase the number of people you're going to speak to and present to this week.
5. Track this on a week-to-week basis, and work for improvement every week.
6. Note all results in your journal.

Advice #9
Keep Yourself Alive

There are those who try to do something new without any errors or failures. They try to bypass problems completely — and they end up losing time, money and pride.

But then there are people who never study or attempt something new at all. Such people really aren't *living* life. They're the type that would rather sit on the bleachers than play the game.

There's an old story about a rich person who was asked how he became rich. As an active and successful person, his answer was straight to the point:

"Two words," he said.

"Yes?"

"Right actions."

"And before that?"

"Wide experience."

"And before that?"

"Wrong actions."

You want to start living?

Get very busy.

Get very active.

Don't be afraid to make some mistakes.

Learn from your mistakes and then get even busier.

You will definitely be *living* — and you will be much more successful!

————————————————

Energy Professionals Perspective

In my first few years in the energy industry helping business owners save on their energy costs, I was always trying to figure out how I could best serve them.

I did have situations where I made mistakes and I knew that I had to improve. There were 2 things that helped me increase my confidence:

1. **Strong mentorship.** I had a few professionals available to me who were willing to listen to my mistakes and instead of ridiculing me or making me feel wrong, they helped look at the mistakes I made from a different viewpoint, and helped me see more workable solutions that would help me and my company grow. This has been a huge part of my success over the past couple decades. I'm always willing to admit I made a mistake, and I'm even more willing to find better solutions for me and my team of professional energy advisors.

2. **Create strong relationships with clients**. Strong relationships allow real communication to occur. Clients know that nobody is perfect, but I've learned that if you admit to your client that you made a mistake, and you have a solution to solve the mistake, nearly all clients are understanding and appreciate your honesty and willingness to improve their situation. Find out what your

client really needs and make sure you do everything to fill that need, including more communication when you make a mistake.

Energy products and services change constantly over the years. Great relationships are the foundation upon which delivering these products and services will rest. If you have strong relationships and great communication with your clients, then the products can be modified and changed in the future to be able to help them achieve their energy efficiency goals and increase their profitability.

"When defeat comes, accept it as a signal that your plans are not sound; rebuild those plans, and set sail once more toward your coveted goal."
— Napoleon Hill, *Think and Grow Rich*

Action Items

1. Write down three mistakes that you may have made in the past.
2. Write down all of the things you learned from them.
3. Write down the different actions that you would take in order to avoid making the same mistakes again. NOTE: If you truly feel you haven't made many mistakes, increase your activity by 10 times, and then repeat this exercise.
4. Note results in your journal.

Advice #10
Avoid the "Hard" Work Trap: Follow Your Passion

A definition of *"hard" work*: doing something you don't enjoy, so you can make enough money to barely survive today and take a vacation sometime in the future, maybe.

Don't fall into the "hard" work trap! If you already have, get out of it!

"I'll do this job just a little longer, and *then* I will start to enjoy my life."

Some people live their whole life working with this idea in mind. This only occurs because a person doesn't love their job. They're just waiting for that happy moment when the hard work is over. The money keeps them going back to the same old grind — but money doesn't have much meaning if a person gets no pleasure from making it.

Here is what Mark Twain said on this subject:

"The law of work does seem utterly unfair — but there it is, and nothing can change it: the higher the pay in enjoyment the worker gets out of it, the higher shall be his pay in cash, too."
— *A Connecticut Yankee in King Arthur's Court*

You can very quickly start to hate your job if you forget why you liked it in the first place and start thinking only about the money you get from it.

Those who do their work with great pleasure will be paid more. And they will spend more effective time getting more successful actions done. They make it look "easy" even though they come to work early and leave late. They do it because they love what they do every day, they are not working for the money! They are working for the love of the game they are playing!

Would you enjoy paying a sales rep who stands dull-faced before you, clearly bored to death with both you and their job? When you could tell that they would be quite happy to leave it all right now if they could?

Have you ever been to a restaurant where the servers don't want to do their jobs? They don't like the profession, they don't like their restaurant, they don't like the customers, and it's obvious to anyone who walks in the door? Unfortunately, there are too many similar examples because this occurs way too often.

Can you think of some *positive* examples you experienced recently? Have you been helped by someone who *loved* their job? They were happy you walked in so they could help you. Did you notice how this attracted your attention? Can you think of the last time you actually *thanked* a sales rep as you paid them for the product or service? Isn't it much nicer to walk away from a sales transaction with a smile on your face and spring in your step?

Love and pleasure from what you do directly influences your ability to have a lot of money without being stressed out.

Many people say this concept is too simple. Luckily for you, though, it is very simple. In fact, that's the whole trick.

Observe for yourself. Look at the "lucky" ones. What do they have in common?

- They love what they're doing all day long.
- They can't wait to get to work in the morning.
- They are the last to leave the office.
- They love their company.
- They love their product or service.
- They have closed contracts waiting for them on Monday morning.

They really are "lucky!"

Jim's Experience

After I got out of the Navy, I was working for the U.S. government in Trident submarine new construction. I hated my job. I hated getting out of bed in the morning. I walked slowly to my office every day. I was getting numb.

One day a friend told me he was making $2,000 a weekend in door-to-door sales. It seemed unbelievable at first, but I was getting desperate about my future. I was nearing 30 and I didn't want to be stuck in a job I hated for the rest of my life. He convinced me to try it. I went out my first Saturday, learned the ropes, loved the product myself and I made $50 an hour. That was *twice as much money* as I made as a professional, licensed nuclear engineer with nearly 7 years of college and post-graduate education.

Unbelievable! The best part was that I had fun talking to people, and the four hours flew by like a warm summer breeze.

I made myself a promise: I would only sell things I would gladly offer to my 85-year old grandmother. If something was good enough for me and my family to use, then I would sell it to others. That has been my guiding principle for over 25 years.

The funny part was that my mom was very upset when I quit my nice, safe, secure, boring government job to be a door-to-door salesman. I told her that I wanted a job that I could have fun doing every day. Her words to me were: *"Oh, honey, work is not fun, it's something hard that you have to do to take care of your family. You can have fun when you retire."*

I love my mom. Years later, when she saw that I was a successful business owner, happily married and had given her two grandsons, she admitted that maybe you could have a high paying job that was fun, too.

Action Items

1. Write down 5 things that you love about helping others from your position.
2. Ask yourself if contributing in this way makes you feel better.
3. Be consistent with executing the things that you love about your job. Note the results in your journal.
4. Decide if you are in the right job now. Then do step 5 and see if you change your mind.
5. In your mind, go back over the last 30 days and spot times when you really did love your job. What made you love your job during those times? Note those results in your journal as well.

Advice #11
What You Actually Offer the Customer

You are basically offering information as a service to the customer. You are not offering the product. You are there to offer information as a service in order to help the customer make the best choice as quickly and efficiently as possible.

Once sold, the product can then be handled or delivered by other people. If the salesperson handles or delivers the product themselves, it is treated as a separate action from the process of the actual sale *("sale" = helping the customer make the best possible choice).*

The process of any sale is often confused with *offering a product and telling the customer to buy it.* When you don't provide the information necessary to making a good decision, and allow the customer the right to choose, you get a very complicated subject called *sales*! This complicated subject requires a lot of advice and "authoritative" opinions on how to "manipulate" and "shove" and "pressure" and "trick" customers into "buying" a product so the company can profit, and the sales rep can make enough money to barely survive.

As a result, we have a public image of a manipulative "salesperson" which is widely spread around the world: smooth, fast talking, high pressure, dishonest, and persistently annoying enough to make people do what they don't want to do: buy something they really didn't want to buy.

Sometimes it appears that the "best" sales reps master the "skills" above. But actually, Champions never sell this way, and they don't advise others to do so either. Those who teach manipulative sales "skills" are actually not able to sell. They have a hard time telling the truth to anyone, including themselves.

Any salesperson taught high-pressure, manipulating sales techniques never deals with the actual customer — they are only dealing with the customer's protest against this sales "technique." This is the cause of high stress and the sense that the salesperson is in a battle "against" the customer — it feels like a war! As a result, we get the feeling that customers don't want to buy, or in general just don't like to talk to sales reps. You have probably heard many salespeople say, "buyers are liars," as they walk away from another failed close.

Nothing mentioned above cancels the main qualities of a Champion: certainty and ability to complete a large number of actions. But this certainty and ability should be directed to giving the customer the *right information to make the best choice*, which actually creates their desire to purchase the product or service. If you press and squeeze the customer, *you* will be pressed and squeezed *by* the customer.

You get people interested in your product or service by being interested in them and their problems, then giving them the information they need and finally, earning their trust.

The rest is easy, if you practice the principles outlined in this book.

Energy Professionals Perspective

When you're helping business decision makers create an energy strategy, you really need to educate the client on what it is that you're doing, so that you can help them make the right decisions.

The first step is to do an energy audit. With this audit, you end up asking dozens of questions regarding their overall energy consumption patterns throughout their specific business model. They may have one large building and many satellite offices, or they could have several large manufacturing plants in multiple locations. The key is to find out. You cannot offer something to this client until you find out what their biggest problems are, what their corporate energy strategy is and what their buying strategy is. If you keep asking the right questions and listen carefully to the answers, you will be able to present a proposal that will be accepted quickly.

Action Items

1. Pick a service or product that you could sell.
2. Write down what questions you would have to ask to find out what they really need.
3. Figure out how you could offer information about that item to a customer, in order to help the customer figure out how to make the best choice as quickly and as efficiently as possible.
4. Repeat the above 2 steps with different items, until you've got an idea that you could actually sell this way.
5. Note the results in your journal.

Advice #12
Never be Afraid to Lose a Customer

This is another hard-and-fast sales rule, and every Champion knows and applies it daily. The highest paid sales reps know this is one of the basic rules of life in sales: you will not have a lot of happy customers if you cling to each prospect, or are afraid to lose them, or are just afraid that they won't buy anything.

This is very important: *you should always be willing and able to just let the customer walk away.* This *doesn't* mean you want them to walk away empty handed. But if you are willing and able to lose a customer, as a rule, you won't lose many of them. In fact, you will have many more customers who refer their friends and associates to you.

The most successful professionals constantly use this rule. Please realize that this is not a trick or intrigue or swindle — it is simple truth.

Champions are not afraid of refusals and they *never* try selling something to somebody who doesn't need their product. That's why they have so many *loyal* customers who constantly refer their friends and associates.

Energy Professionals Perspective

I'm sure you have walked into a restaurant and noticed a sign on the wall that read:

We reserve the right to refuse service to anyone.

Sometimes you will find yourself working with a client that has an abrasive personality, or that is asking for things that are inconsistent with your personal beliefs or business philosophy.

Potentially compromising your integrity or working with someone with whom you have a bad relationship, is something you should never have to do. You always have the right to refuse service to anyone who is rude, abusive or unethical. You should never feel you have to act unethically to make a sale.

Whenever you find a person you're talking to is someone you really would <u>not</u> want to create a long-term relationship with, you *always* have the option of not continuing the sales process with them. You can excuse yourself and either recommend that someone else from your company provide that service, or if you feel it would just be a bad relationship for the firm as a whole, just thank them for their time and hospitality and be willing to walk away as politely as possible.

Always remember that you have the power of choice regarding the prospects that you work with and choose to serve. Remember that your reputation in the industry is important. Even though you may not choose to work with someone, you should still treat them with respect and dignity. Choose the high road in any potential relationship, and don't get flustered when making a decision that a relationship would best be serviced by somebody else. It is bad business to spread bad news about others, and that includes co-workers and clients. You can explain to your manager why you chose not to work with a specific client, but don't spread bad news about the client to other clients. You don't have to tell a client you refuse to work with their decision maker. Companies change executives and managers all the time. You will find in the future that decision makers change and now there is somebody in charge of purchasing that you can work with and keep your integrity intact.

You're the one who decides the type of business that you want, and your relationships should reflect that.

Action Items

1. List out 5 qualities of a customer who you would *not* want to work with.
2. List out 5 qualities of a great customer who you *would* want to work with.
3. Tune your mind to look for the qualities that *you* want in a relationship. You'll find that you'll end up attracting those people as long as you're specific in the definition of those qualities.
4. Track and note the results in your journal.

Advice #13
Never Forget You're the Swan, Not the Ugly Duckling

Let's assume you have a product of high quality and a corresponding high price.

Salespeople are constantly pounded on by customers with a simple phrase: "It's too expensive!" This is normal! Welcome to the sales profession. Customers always say, "It costs too much!" Having heard this too many times, and too often failing to prove that it's *not* too expensive, the salesperson may start to believe *every* customer is going to say this.

So, they train themselves to be ready for it. They literally prepare for the "war" with every customer — pretending to be friendly, but ready to fight at a moment's notice. They don't keep their attention on all their product benefits, and instead prepare to do battle against all the drawbacks including the "high price." As soon as they start thinking this way, there are no more advantages in their mind, just rebuttals against the expected objections.

Hans Christian Andersen's The Ugly Duckling *is still an appropriate story today. The "ugly duckling" was actually a baby swan. But the ducks and geese made him believe that he was no good and he didn't belong anywhere. What did that ugly duckling decide when he came up to the lake and saw the other swans? "They will probably kill me because I'm so ugly... Well... Let them..."*

The same is true with a salesperson. Everything is basically fine with them; they are smart and competent. But without the actual sales skills fully understood and drilled to perfection, they don't believe that everything is fine, and they go to each customer with this attitude: "I will have to prove it to them, or I'll fail!"

Even experienced salespeople can act like this - suffering from not knowing just how good their product or service is. They listened to their failed prospects and other average sales reps tell them how bad it is, how expensive it is and how they are never going to be successful selling it.

The best way to fully handle this phenomenon is for salespeople to act like professionals, and train so well that they know all the benefits and advantages of their product or service and constantly. They *systematically* prove, to their own satisfaction, all the benefits and successes of the customers who have used their product or service.

Training and practice *are* how Champion sales reps are made. And they never forget they are *swans*.

Energy Professionals Perspective

Being an excellent consultant in the energy industry requires that you are constantly up to date with the latest developments in the industry. There are many things that we are required to know from the standpoint of regulatory changes, product features, market trends, supplier pricing options and new energy efficiency products that we must constantly stay current with.

By doing things such as continuing education and also by working on improving your own abilities within our industry, you will become more valuable as a professional energy advisor to your colleagues and your customers.

Make sure that you have a well-defined personal improvement plan so that you can increase your competence and ability — not only in a professional capacity but also in the areas of communication, human interaction and building relationships. These are valuable skillsets that will allow you to build a prosperous future as a professional advisor in any field.

"The big challenge is to become all that you have the possibility of becoming. You cannot believe what it does to the human spirit to maximize your human potential and stretch yourself to the limit."
— *Jim Rohn*

Action Items

1. Find out what your employer offers for continuous professional education. Work out a scheduled amount of time per week that you're going to spend on increasing your skills and ability to serve your clients and colleagues in the energy industry.
2. Work out 5 areas that you would like to improve in, and the action items you're going to take to start improving in those areas right away.
3. Record the above plans in your journal and track your progress as you go.

Advice #14
How to Be a Wealthy Sales Champion

Have you ever been completely enthusiastic about a new idea?

How do you feel about it? How do you talk about it?

You should be ready to talk for hours about:

- Your product or service
- How it's manufactured
- Its benefits
- How to use it
- About your company and how it was founded
- Any other interesting details about your product

Your product and your company should *inspire* you. You should be able to be completely *enthusiastic* about them. You should be *dedicated* to your product, your company and your job. You should be *interested* in your profession every day. You should be willing to be a professional, which requires study and practice. This is what it really takes to be a Champion in your field.

Only after you have decided that you like your own product, service and company, will any other sales techniques really work for long-term success.

Learning techniques in order to sell a product you *don't like* will ultimately lead to you hating your product, your job and even your profession. You will "push away" more customers than you attract.

If you can't develop passion for your product and company, if you don't believe in the value of your product, you will tend to limit your own pay, whether you are aware of this principle or not. And you will tend to attract customer objections, even if they didn't have any objections in the first place.

In order to be a wealthy sales Champion, you have to sell a product you believe in and work for a company you can be proud of. It's your choice what you sell and who you work for. Choose wisely. Your success and happiness in this profession depend on your choice.

Also, you can take responsibility for improving your product and your company. That may take more courage. It's up to you.

Action Items

1. Write down 10 things regarding your skillset that you're passionate about, that you want to share with others. Note any resultant thoughts in your journal.
2. Write down 5 things you like most about the products/services you are offering to your clients.
3. Write down 5 things that make you proud of your company.
4. Note how this could help you be more professional and successful.

Part 2: Prospecting

> "Just keep talking to a *lot* of different people, and talking to warm prospects more frequently. Keep honoring their right 'to choose,' and then help them to decide 'to buy or not to buy.' If the decision is 'to buy,' then help them decide 'what exactly' to buy. If the customer decides *not* to buy, respect that decision. Don't assume the door is closed forever, and keep finding ways to help them understand what they really need and show them how to get it."
> — Andrey Sizov

Advice #15
Be Friendly and Engaging with People You Meet

The goal of the wealthy and successful Sales Champion is *NOT* trying to high pressure close every single potential customer, hunting them down and forcing them into a decision without their understanding and agreement.

The real goal is *easy*!

Just keep talking to a *lot* of different people and keep talking to warm prospects more frequently. Honor their right "to choose," and then help them to decide "to buy or not to buy." If the decision is "to buy," then help them decide "what exactly" to buy. If the customer decides *not* to buy, respect that decision. Don't assume the door is closed forever. Keep finding ways to help them understand what products or services really fill their needs and then show them how you can help them. Here's the real secret — it's a never-ending process. You keep talking to more and more people and find the warm prospects, keep all your appointments on time, keep helping them understand how you can help them, and then keep talking to more people. There is no limit to the number of people you can talk to. The more appointments you make, the more future success you create for yourself and your company.

A sales rep that clings desperately to each and every potential customer (trying to be "liked" by them) will accumulate a lot of internal negativity and will eventually stop trying completely.

Real success means willingness to talk to more and more people.

Andrey's Coat Collar

In 1988 I was going through ship commander training and I needed to get a rare lambskin collar for my overcoat. Real Russian naval officers were incredibly competent and willing to do any job in any climate, with complete disregard for any barriers or regulations. And *real* Russian naval officers were also the most classy and stylish rogues imaginable. In short, real Russian naval officers wore rare lambskin collars — banned by regulations — which meant I really had to have one.

I went to every tailor in St Petersburg. Not one of them offered that collar. This was a big problem for a young man looking to fit the role of a real Russian naval officer.

Luckily, I mentioned my problem to a real estate agent, who taught me the first target of a Sales Champion:

<u>Everybody</u> *must know that you are selling (or buying) something!*

Everybody must know that you have something valuable to offer. I thought it would be weird and uncomfortable to tell everybody I met that I needed a rare collar for my naval overcoat. As if he read my mind, my real estate agent friend said: "Yes, this is the biggest problem for salespeople — considering the action of talking to very many people uncomfortable and embarrassing."

"It simply means that *everybody* must know what you do. *You continue talking to many, many people, and keep looking for the best ways to introduce what you do.* You will get better and better at it. Just remember the trick is to get people curious about what you are doing."

I applied this principle to my problem. I told all my friends and acquaintances what I was looking for; some thought I was crazy and laughed at me and others had no idea how to help me.

Finally, I told my mom and her friends. She looked at me and asked if I was aware that she was a chief economist at a respectable company, and neither she nor her respectable friends had any interest at all in collars and navy coats. So, I told those "respectable" ladies a story. I explained the difference between staff navy officers (those who never had to go to sea) and real Russian naval officers, who actually went to sea and chased American submarines around the North Atlantic, and why it was a matter of honor to wear this special collar. They became curious and started asking questions.

If your story is interesting, people will listen to you. People love interesting stories, and telling stories allows you to attract more attention to your project.

After 2 days of telling everyone I saw about the special collar I was looking for, I started to receive advice from many different people, including people I had never even met.

After 2 weeks of telling my story to everyone, a man I met on a train the very first day I applied this lesson called and told me he had found a place that sold the special collar I needed. I thanked him, bought the collar and proudly wore it to show everyone I was a "real" Russian naval officer.

Energy Professionals Perspective

Having a two-minute story to introduce your main product or service will help you overcome the fear of talking to everyone and allow you to be friendly and engaging.

This is something you have to practice and be willing to improve constantly. Also, it helps to have a couple short interesting success stories handy to bring to the conversation.

Many people ask me what I do, and I have practiced that answer a thousand times and it has continued to evolve over the years. I always make sure my answer is short, to the point and interesting. And then, depending on who I'm talking to, I have several different short stories that highlight the success one of my clients enjoyed using our consulting firm.

I never wait for someone to ask me what I do. When I have a chance, I tell them what my company does.

My simple opening is nearly always the same: "We save businesses millions of dollars on their energy spend every year." That simple statement usually prompts the question: "How?" Then I tell a couple of my favorite customer success stories. And people remember me and sometimes weeks, months or even years later, they call and ask me for help with their energy-related problems.

Action Items

1. Write down 5 potential prospects that could be interested in your product, service or opportunity.
2. Write down your own 2-minute story that you would use with each of those 5 people.
3. Practice those over and over again until you feel confident you could approach them with those words.
4. Call all of them and see how it goes.
5. Listen carefully to the responses and correct your story as needed.
6. Keep track of this exercise and its results in your journal.

Advice #16
Overcome Scarcity

One of the things that everyone needs to be aware of, coming into the energy industry — or any other business — is that you have to have enough prospects to talk to.

The first question you need to ask yourself is: "Who are the potential customers that would be interested in my products and services?"

The first thing you have to overcome is the concept of scarcity. Many times, we look around and we think, "I don't have enough people to talk to!"

Then you need to qualify your target market. Does your company have a residential product or service? What parts of the country are you able to service? What types of businesses are you able and willing to work with? Fortune 500? Fortune 5000? Every business, no matter what size?

Once you identify your target market, you need to find or buy a list of potential customers. Ideally you want an initial list to be as large as possible. Millions of prospects are much better than thousands. When you realize there are literally millions of potential customers in North America alone, the idea of "scarcity" starts to disappear.

When you look at the potential list of businesses in your target market, you can then narrow down that list to customers who fit your ideal profile, such as annual revenue, numbers of buildings, franchises, corporate headquarters, etc.

Now the work begins. You need to reach as many of these ideal prospects as quickly as possible and build your warm prospect list.

This is a numbers game. If you only call or email 10 leads from your list each day, you may get a response. If you reach out to 50 or 100 leads per day you will definitely get positive responses, and you definitely will not believe there is a scarcity of people to introduce to your product or service.

If you can do email and social media marketing (LinkedIn has been very successful for business to business transactions), you increase the number of decision makers who are familiar with you and your product.

But do NOT wait for some marketing miracle to bring you warm prospects. Your direct effort will be far more successful at creating your own customer base. Marketing can add to this for sure but don't wait for someone else to bring you a warm prospect, go out and create your own prospects!

Every day you should have a "line-up" of warm & hot prospects. Warm is interested and asking more questions and gathering more data to prepare for the close and delivery of your product/service.

Hot is a customer where all the questions have been answered and you are ready for the contract to be approved and signed.

Your line-up is your direct indicator of success. If you have two customers on your line-up, you are going to feel the scarcity, and even worse, you may start to high pressure those two prospects and you may even get angry with them. This leads to internal stress for you and the customer. This leads to lower success rates and lower customer satisfaction!

If you have 20 warm & hot prospects on your list, with actions listed out to move them closer to signing up with you, you are going to feel the positivity of abundance. You will take more time to make sure all the buying questions are answered fully, and your stress level is low, and even more importantly, the customer satisfaction level is HIGH!

And if you want to be a Champion, never stop prospecting!

Action Items

Answer the following question: Do you feel that you come from a mindset of scarcity, or a mindset of abundance?

A *scarcity mindset* can be identified by the feeling of, "I don't have anybody to talk to," or "I need more leads." If you answer the above question for yourself and find that you have a scarcity mindset:

1. Go to a crowded place such as a mall or downtown area.
2. Walk around and just look at people. In your mind, create potential conversations you could have with them.
3. Keep walking around and performing this exercise until you realize that there are a lot of people to talk to.
4. Note the results in your journal.

Advice #17
Broaden Your Point of View Regarding Prospects

Whenever I go out and I'm in a social situation — whether it's going to the store, attending a party, or just riding on a plane — I realize that everyone around me knows someone that may have a problem my company can solve.

Sometimes the problem is a personal issue, and just by listening to the person patiently and letting them know I care is enough to help them solve their own problem. One of the great things about people in general is that when you genuinely listen to their needs and you help them in some way, they normally want to return the favor.

A great example of this was a friend who introduced me to one his colleagues. We hit it off instantly, and at that time, she did not know anyone who needed our energy advisory services, but we stayed in touch. One day out of the blue, she called me and introduced me to one of her friends in the Midwest. She had a connection to a new CEO of a large manufacturing plant. She introduced us to him, and my VP was able to save his company nearly a million dollars on his natural gas usage. It was a big win for our company as well as solving a big problem for the customer. It turned out that our major competitors were trying to talk to this CEO for two years unsuccessfully.

We constantly recruit referral partners to introduce us to companies that may be hard to contact any other way. And you never know where your next big opportunity will come from as long as you continue to tell people what problems you can solve.

"If you want to be a fantastic business success:

1. *Make a friend.*
2. *Solve a problem.*
3. *Ask for and expect referrals."*

— Greg Kapp
Advisory Board Member, All for One Foundation

Action Items

1. Make a decision right now to look at ways to help people solve problems wherever you go. By providing that value, you'll be able to expand your prospect list and your markets immensely.
2. Note the results in your journal.

Part 3: Research

"Knowledge is Power"

This is such an old saying that there are arguments about who said it first in the past thousand years. But it's true. The more you know about a particular subject, the more ability you have to succeed in that subject. If you want to fly a small plane, you don't just go to the airport, hop in the front seat and take off. Everyone knows you have to take a class and flying lessons from a pro. Why is it any different in sales? You learn as much about your products and services as you can learn, and you keep learning more as long as you want to be a Champion. Before you go to meet with a customer, take a few minutes or hours and learn more about that customer! There has never been a time when it was easier to find out about companies and people than it is today. We live in a world where Siri or Alexa is at our service to answer any question, we wish to ask, 24 hours a day. There is simply no excuse today to meet with a prospect without doing some research first.

You want to be successful? Know before you go!

Jim@KnowledgeisPower.Today

Advice #18
Be Prepared

When going into a new presentation within the energy industry, you should be well-prepared for your presentation.

Everyone has a very specific and unique set of circumstances that applies to their particular situation. By being prepared, you respect *their* time, respect *your* time, and wind up being a position where you have everything well-structured to improve their situation and condition.

So do your research and preparation both before you go into your initial interviews with your clients, and when you're coming back to actually help them implement their plan. Make sure you have a very clear picture of what it is that you're presenting so that you can have a successful implementation meeting for that particular client.

Action Items

1. On a scale of 1 - 10, rate yourself on how effective you've been on preparing to talk to new prospects.
2. On a scale of 1 - 10, rate yourself on how prepared you've been for the presentation of the product or services you are planning on implementing.
3. Unless you're a 10 on all of these, write down 5 ways you can improve upon them in order to be able to be more prepared and able to provide a substantial amount of value to your clients in the future.
4. Note these in your journal and track your progress with them.

Advice #19
Look at Your Presentation Through the Eyes of the Customer

Review your presentation from the perspective of the client.

Many times, sales reps will go in and just sell the product that *they* want to sell. If you don't view your product through the eyes of the customer, you could completely miss the mark. Most incapable or unprofessional salespeople are just trying to jam things down the throats of their clients.

The problem is, if you can't see how it's going to improve their situation, it puts you on very unstable ground. You want to present your product from a very stable position. By taking a moment and looking at what you're about to present, through the eyes of your prospect, it will allow you to really create a tremendous sense of empathy when you're sitting with them. It will result in your better understanding their situation. They will appreciate your presentation that much more.

Take the time to look at the company's website, their LinkedIn profile, their top executives' profiles and any recent press releases. This will greatly help you understand your prospect better and you will have a better closing ratio because you take the time to see things through their eyes.

Action Items

1. Rate yourself on a scale of 1 - 10 on how you've been at looking at the situation from your prospect's viewpoint.
2. Write down 3 ways that you can better prepare yourself and assume their point of view when going in to present something to them.
3. Track and note the results in your journal.

Part 4: Contact

> *"If you are willing to spend enough time and effective action letting everyone know you have a good product, you will win."*
> *— Jim Mathers*

Advice #20
Winners Take Action

Who becomes a winner in this world? Anyone who is <u>willing</u> to take *more action*, complete *more effective steps*, talk to *more people*, help *more people* solve problems and *persist as long as it takes* to reach the goal they dream up.

The conclusion is very simple. You will win if you act, and act, and act, and never quit taking effective actions that move you in the direction of your goal.

Maybe you already know this. Maybe you think only the *quality* of your action is important. But, very often the reason for failure in any activity is simply *not enough* action taken, no matter how great the quality of the product or service is.

There's an old saying: "Build a better mousetrap, and the world will beat a path to your door." Popular though this saying may be, it's actually not true. There are countless businesses and sales reps that have failed because they were "waiting" for people to come and buy their high-quality products.

To be truly successful, you must have a good quality product or service. But if you spend most of your time trying to make it perfect, and too little time and action letting people know you have a good product, you will fail.

The truth is simple: *if you are willing to spend enough time and effective action letting everyone know you have a good product, you will win.*

Energy Professionals Perspective

In my experience, I find that in today's hectic world, with endless to-do lists and action plans, there can appear to be an overwhelming amount of work to do. One of the things that can paralyze a great energy advisor is being overwhelmed with incomplete actions on their to-do list.

Even more paralyzing is holding all of your action list items in your brain on a day-to-day basis.

There is an old Chinese proverb that says: *"If someone is cupping their hands, and their hands are full of rotten rice, they cannot receive new, fresh rice until they empty their hands."*

The same goes for you in your daily activities: in order for you to receive a lot of new things, you have to wrap up and finish the old things.

"All you can do is all you can do — but all you can do is enough!"
— Art Williams

Action Items

1. Take 1 hour, undistracted, and sit down and write down all the things you have not completed. You will be amazed sometimes to find your list is not as long as it seemed when you were carrying it around in your head.
2. Work out what you're going to do over the next week in order to be able to complete those actions or move them to the next step in the process of a longer project you're working on. Also, if you have listed actions that are no longer needed, get them off the list.
3. Make it a regular part of your week to "empty your hands" in order to receive many new things.
4. This often works like magic -- because your mindset is better, and you feel less mentally cluttered, you can wind up having an abundance of positive activity coming your way.
5. Keep track of the results of this exercise in your journal.

Advice #21
Don't Be Stopped by Failure or "Fear" of Failure

To fully understand how thinking about potential failure can cut down your willingness to act in a certain area, let's look at two types of responses to your proposal.

First type: You tell people about your product. They not only refuse to buy from you, but also make antagonistic remarks about you, your information, your company or your product. They are not happy that you showed up at all and they make that very clear to you.

How willing are you to keep talking with these customers?

Second type: You tell people about your product. They don't always buy your product, but they're always glad to see you, they think your product information is very interesting and they make positive remarks about your proposal even if they don't buy right then.

How willing are you to keep talking with *these* customers?

Which type of customer are you willing to be more persistent with? Which type of customer do you think you will be happy and successful with?

Here is the main secret: *people's attitude toward you, your presence and your proposals, will ultimately depend on* **your attitude** *only*.

Rule: *You can* always *positively influence the customer's attitude. Learn this secret and you will be more successful, happier to come to work every day, and if you persist long enough, you will become a Champion.*

Jim's Experience in Virginia

I was running a door-to-door sales crew one night in northern Virginia. There were some "old-timers" and some brand-new sales reps I was training. I was handing out maps of the territories each rep was to work that night, and one of the old-timers pointed at one map and said, "That neighborhood is terrible!"

Another experienced rep agreed, saying that nobody ever bought anything from anyone in that crummy neighborhood. I took this as a challenge to prove the main point of this advice: *"You can always positively influence your customer's attitude."*

I informed all the reps that there were no bad neighborhoods. I took the map for that area and issued a challenge to all the other sales reps: I would take the "crummy neighborhood" and make twice as many sales as they would.

Three hours later, we met back up, and I had a dozen sales. They shook their heads in disbelief. Nobody else had more than six. My positive attitude "infected" the crummy neighborhood. I talked to a lot of interesting people. They didn't all buy from me, but everyone was nice to me.

"I never see failure as failure, but only as a learning experience."
— Tom Hopkins

Action Items: Influencing Customer Attitude

1. Decide you're bored and don't really want to talk to anybody. Now, go up and talk to someone. Note how they act.
2. Now decide you feel really good today. Go up to another person and talk to them. Note how they act.
3. Repeat the above 2 steps until you can clearly see how your attitude affects how people talk to you.
4. Note the results in your journal.

Action Items: Learning from Failure

1. Look back at 3 failures you feel you've had in your career.
2. Look back at what you learned from them.
3. Realize that failures are only failures if you don't learn from them.
4. Note the results in your journal.

Advice #22
Daily Drilling for Success

If you were an elite athlete and you didn't do warm-up exercises first, you could do tremendous damage to your body and (more importantly) your ability to perform as an athlete during the competition. You could pull muscles, tear ligaments, and just not perform as well as you should be able to.

You could waste a lot of time worrying over making phone calls to prospects: "What's going to happen?" and "What are they going to say?" or "What crazy objection that I can't handle are they going to throw at me this time?"

The scenarios we create in our own minds are usually far worse that what happens in real life.

A pro athlete doesn't simply spring onto the court with no warm-up, no practice shots, no stretching. In a similar way, it always boggled my mind that people would just jump into making phone calls right from a cold start, without any kind of warm up.

A method we have used for years that is very successful is to pair up with another sales rep and before you start calling prospects, you drill each other alternately. Start off being interested in each other's full pitch for the first couple times so you each get smoother at delivering the basic idea of your product, then spend a few minutes giving each other your toughest objections, and you will be amazed at how relaxed you get and how you find out new ways to handle objections. Make sure you drill with different people each day so you can learn to handle different attitudes.

15 minutes of drilling every morning with co-workers before trying to make that first call makes all the difference in the world in your confidence and your attitude. If you don't have a co-worker, call a friend or relative and drill your script with them! It really works!

Action Items

1. If your company already has this daily procedure in place, then do this every day with the knowledge that you will get better and so will your teammates that you drill with.
2. If you are by yourself, call some people who like you enough to want you to succeed, and drill with them until you feel really comfortable.
3. Look at your prospect list. Decide on at least 20 prospect calls you're going to make today and call those people. Help them take their next step whether it's a meeting, getting questions answered, preparing the contract pricing, etc.
4. Note the results in your journal.

Advice #23
Having Real Conversations

Do your best to have real conversations with the people you interact with daily. This does not mean just "gate-keepers," prospects or "decision makers." We mean referral partners, brokers, co-workers, juniors and management at work; and family & friends outside your work environment are included as well.

Generally speaking, people are not having "real" conversations. Most people have acceptable social responses they automatically use to answer most questions. If you can recognize this, you'll be able to break through and have real conversations with people.

The most commonly recognized social response is heard every day:
Q: "How are you doing?"
Social Answer: "Great! How are you?"

When I start to talk to a large group of people, I'll ask: "How are you doing today?"
20 to 30% percent respond: "Great!"
I always pause a moment and then ask:
"How are the rest of you doing?!"
That cracks the social defense and people start to laugh & relax, and they know that I'm really interested in all of them.

Personally, when someone tells me they are doing "great" – I look and listen carefully to see if I can tell if they are really happy, bored or upset. If they are really happy, I ask what just happened in their life, and then they usually launch into their latest success. If they are bored or upset, I ask: "How are you really doing?" And they realize I'm really interested in them, and they tell me what's really happening in their life.

I know, some of you are thinking right now:

"I don't have time to listen to everyone's story."

I can only tell you that if you go through life giving and accepting only shallow social responses, you are going to miss out on some of the most interesting stories you ever heard. And when it comes to sales and consulting, if you cannot crack that social defense, you won't hear about what your competition is offering; you won't find out what the real problem is; you won't find out who the "real" decision maker is; and you won't build a "real" relationship with this prospect.

Remember, you never close a "company," but you can build relationships with the "people" who work for companies.

Being successful in any type of sales means that you have to be able to cut through the social defense system and have a real conversation with a prospect. You'll see it and feel it when someone starts to trust you and becomes willing to open up and really talk to you. You'll find out the real story and then you'll be able to deliver a much more powerful & effective presentation.

Nick's Take: Getting "What They Really Think"

It can be a real problem in a sales cycle to get from someone what they really think, yet without that, the sale is not likely to happen. The main problem I've seen is that sales reps just aren't interested enough in the prospect to get through the social defenses. They're too focused on the close or trying to educate the prospect before they're ready to listen. You have to build trust.

The definition of trust that I use: *someone willing to tell you what they really think*. And getting that to happen requires a high degree of interest on the salesperson's part.

As an energy advisor, most of your commercial prospects have many other problems to deal with besides their energy bills. One of the first things you need to uncover is WHO are you really supposed to be talking to in that company who will be your main point of contact and who will really take the time to listen to you — and only then will you be having a real conversation.

When you can do that as a sales rep or consultant, you're different than any other sales rep the prospect has ever met. To them you're not even a "sales" rep because a "sales" rep is someone they've had a bad experience with, in the past. They consider you a friend, mentor, consultant or *someone who is truly there to help them*. They need a real, genuine, caring professional to listen, understand and guide them to a solution.

Be interested and show it. The key to getting someone to continue telling you about their needs in more detail is to be interested and to fully understand and acknowledge what they say. As they reveal more and more, you're in a real conversation. Note: if they say something you don't understand, don't just skip it! Ask them to explain more about the point you didn't understand. If you don't clarify what they said, it can cause problems for you later if it turns out to be a very important issue to the customer.

Part of having that real conversation is when they reveal a company goal, issue or problem, to *always* ask a prospect, "How long have you been thinking about that?" It's almost always a long time. The reason for asking this question is that when you get all the way to the close and they say, "We need to think about it," you can point out how long they've already been thinking about it and pretty much collapse that objection. This is fully explained in advice #57.

The sales rep or consultant who's truly successful is genuinely caring and interested enough to get the full truth about what problem or problems the company really needs to handle.

Action Items:

1. Have a "social" communication with someone. Pick someone such as a spouse or a family member, or someone within your own team. Just have a social communication: "Hi! How are you?" "Fine!" "How about those Giants?" and so on.
2. Now sit down in a distraction-free environment and have a real conversation with that person. Find out what they're really thinking. Ask them about their hopes, their dreams. What are they trying to achieve? Continue asking until you know they're totally willing to share what they think.
3. Note the results in your journal.

Part 5: Interview

> "You discuss these positive qualities with the customer, solely in terms of the future use and potential benefit *to the customer*. How will your customer use the product or service to improve their life? The lack of understanding this important benefit often misleads both customer and salesperson. Why do people buy anything? So they can use it for their benefit!"
> — Jim Mathers

Advice #24
Understand the Customer's Viewpoint on Quality

What is "quality" from the viewpoint of the customer? Simply put, how does the customer decide if your product is bad or good?

The perception of quality of products or services is based on the degree of satisfying the customer's *expectations*.

Did they get what they expected? Did they get exactly what they wanted? Did they get what they were promised by you? Any product has to "look good" to the customer at the time they buy it, but it also has to perform some useful function for the person after they get home. The suit fits perfectly in the store, but it should continue to fit perfectly for a long time after; it should be easy to clean and look good when it's pulled out of the suitcase on a business trip.

The same holds true with furniture, and for any other product or service. It should continue to provide good value to the customer after they use it for a while. What does "good value" mean for your customer in the long run? How do you prevent complaints or returns?

A tremendous amount of complaints and customer dissatisfaction occurs for two main reasons:

1. The sales rep didn't find out what value the customer expected from using the product or service.

2. The sales rep promised more benefits than the product or service actually delivers.

What are the features or benefits this particular customer

expects when they use it? This becomes the exact reason many sales aren't made in the first place! The customer can't trust a sales rep who doesn't show that they care about how the customer is going to use the product or service in the future and doesn't take the time to really find out what the customer expects from that product or service. Even worse; if there was a promised benefit that is not delivered, it will make the product or service look bad, the company look bad and it will be one more bad experience that customer has with sales reps in general.

One of the tests I use for this is very simple: If I run into to one of my customers a year from now, would they invite me into their office or out to lunch? Would they be very happy to see me? Or not? If you can confidently predict that your customers will want to greet you warmly a year from now, then you are doing things that right and this will lead to long-term sales success.

Action Items

1. Pick out a product or service that you sell, or that you could potentially sell.
2. Put together a list of questions you could ask a prospect for this product or service, that would definitely tell you (as well as demonstrate to your customer) the benefits the customer will expect from that product or service.
3. Track and note the results in your journal.

Advice #25
Be the Financial Advisor

A financial advisor is a person you are willing to take important advice from, such as, "How should I invest my hard-earned savings?" This is a *trusted advisor* that people feel comfortable asking for advice when they are in doubt about a financial service or product.

As a result of many surveys, we found that a great *trusted advisor* has 4 main qualities from the *customer's* viewpoint:

- *This person is on my side. They are interested in my future benefit.*
- *This person is an expert in the subject being discussed.*
- *This person finds out exactly what my problems are, and they understand what I need.*
- *They will not force me to make a fast decision; they will make sure I have the information I need and will allow me to decide for myself and make the best choice for me.*

If a customer feels that the sales rep has the above qualities, they consider this rep as *a trusted advisor*. Then, at the moment of making a decision, the customer listens to the sales rep's advice. If this trust is not created, the customer will *not* listen to the sales rep, will go off to *think about it*.

Once again, it all goes back to *benefits*. Yes, these valuable qualities only exist if the sales rep concentrates on benefits for the customer. The benefits will become obvious when the customer begins to use what they bought. If the sales rep wants to make sure that the customer will be happy with the results of using that product or service, the rep will take an interest in emphasizing the future value while talking with the customer.

And the problem of "What questions should I ask to find out what the customer really wants?" will not exist. This problem only exists when a sales rep actually just wants to ask: "Well, are you going to buy this or not?" or "When are you going to pay?" This is never the Champion's attitude. It results in uncomfortable silence or meaningless chatter and worst of all, a dissatisfied customer.

Anybody will answer questions about topics that they find interesting. It's much easier to show the true qualities of a product or service when you get the customer talking about what interests them, and if you show that you are truly interested in the customer's future benefit. Champions realize quickly when the customer is not interested in the sales pitch and they immediately start asking questions to find out what the customer *is* interested in. Customers are *never* interested in the sales rep's problems or commission.

True product quality and value becomes visible *only* in use. The proof of a good sales rep is a low complaint percentage, along with a high referral rate after the sale. The sales rep must always understand the true long-term quality and value of their product or service and must be willing to continue to direct the customer's attention to the long-term benefits and value. When this is done correctly, there is no question of selling your product or service at a discount or arguing over price.

"Life is made up not necessarily of great sacrifices or high-level duties but of little things. The smiles, the kindnesses, the commitments and obligations and responsibilities that are given habitually and lovingly are the blessings that win and preserve the heart and bring comfort to oneself as well as to others. This is the ministry of service performed by every useful life." — Sir John Templeton

Advice #26
Listen!

Regarding sales, there are three abilities that distinguish professionals from amateurs:

1. The skill of asking proper questions.

2. The skill of *really listening* to a customer, not interrupting them and not finishing their sentences or thoughts when they pause to think.

3. The skill of utilizing the customer's answers to explain simply and honestly how the product will benefit them in the long-term.

Energy Professionals Perspective

A common concept that I've heard for many years is, "You've got two ears and one mouth. Use them in the correct proportion." Being able to listen is one of the primary keys to be a great consultant.

Make sure that you take the time to listen and really find out what your prospect needs in order to improve their situation.

Part of being a good listener means that you are sincerely interested in what the person has to say. If you find yourself thinking about what *you're* going to say next, you're not really listening anymore. People that start planning what their responses will be while the other person is still talking have functionally left the conversation. You can actually ruin a conversation this way, because no matter what you may think; a person can perceive when you've "checked out" of the conversation, and on some level they are going to be offended.

Make sure that you're listening, and that you are sincerely interested in what the other person has to say. It is a skill you can learn, and it can be improved if you take the time to practice. Don't be "fake" in your interest because *anyone* can sense when you are.

"While we're talking, let me offer you some free advice: talk less, smile more."
— Aaron Burr (character) from *Hamilton: An American Musical*

Action Items

1. On a scale of 1 - 10, how good have you been at listening to the other person?
2. What could you do differently in order to be more interested and be a better listener in the future?
3. Drill this with a friend or co-worker and ask them to be honest with you while you're drilling this skill.
4. Note your answers in your journal.

Advice #27
Set the Next Meeting

Champions know exactly what to pay attention to. This is what makes them the best.

No matter what you sell, there is always a common denominator of any sale. You always sell exactly one thing, always, no matter what else is going on. Whatever the result of the meeting, the main thing you have to sell is *the next meeting or contact*.

Professionals know that the next meeting is much, much more important than just "getting paid right now."

Get that next meeting lined up, even if it's a follow-up call after the close.

The more prospects you talk to and the more times you talk to the same prospect, the more loyal customers you will create.

Energy Professionals Perspective

In the energy industry, scheduling the next meeting is extremely important. If you're doing a multi-step presentation where you have to do the research and then come back and present the product that you're going to sell, then you have to have that next meeting set at the conclusion of the first meeting.

Once your client is a happy customer in your book of clients, then you need to set up follow-up meetings. These can be anywhere from quarterly to annually, depending on your relationship and expectations with that client.

The value of the next meeting cannot be stressed enough. That next meeting being set will result in more referrals *and* more products and services being sold to that same client in the future.

Action Items

1. On a scale of 1 - 10, how good have you been at setting the next appointment?
2. Drill this with a friend or co-worker until you never forget to set the next appointment.
3. Note your answers in your journal.

Advice #28
When Selling: Act Like *You*

Have you been taught to sell by learning to say or do things that you would never do naturally? Have you been taught to just memorize a script and pretend to be someone or something you are not?

If so, you will find yourself under continual stress at your job. You will never earn a lot of money if you are constantly stressed out!

Rule: *Be yourself! Learn to talk to people pleasantly, naturally, like you do with your friends. Apply that same natural communication in sales. You and your customers will have more fun communicating with each other.*

Learn to communicate easily and watch your commissions multiply!

Older sales schools had a passion for "tricks" and unusual solutions for getting customers to say "yes" whether they really wanted the product or not. These "tricks" have given the honorable profession of sales a bad name and have left a sour taste in the mouth of many customers. These tricks were born from a misunderstanding of the basic truths of sales.

Like any profession, there are basic truths that are very simple to learn and lead to consistent results. If you understand them, and *practice* them honestly, you will become a very competent sales professional. If you continue to practice and improve, you will become a sales Champion.

The sales profession is one of the highest paid professions

in the world! But why is it that 20 percent of the sales reps make 80 percent of the sales? Because 80 percent of all sales reps tend to complicate the whole process and end up with bad results, upset customers, a lot of stress, and too little commission.

The "lucky" ones seem to always be at the top of the commission scale. But it's not "luck."

The best sales professionals truly understand, practice and apply the basic principles of sales consistently. When these basic truths are known and applied, it looks like "magic" or "luck." Anyone can learn the basics and become a professional, and with enough practice, a Champion.

How do champion sports teams continue to be champions? Is it just luck? Is it just money? *No*! They practice the fundamentals over and over, day after day. Professional athletes spend much more time practicing than they do actually playing the game.

Do you want to be a Champion? Be honest with yourself.

If your answer is yes, then you must decide to practice your professional skills until they are easy to do. With practice, these fundamental truths become part of your normal daily actions. You will start to apply the basic principles without having to stop and think about what to do or say to help the customer make a choice and close the deal.

And the best part is, if you are willing to practice and become a Champion, you and your customer are happy and you *both win*. No stress, no strain, for you or the customer, and you help the customer achieve what they want, and you make *much* higher commissions consistently.

These basic truths apply to any type of sale; on the phone,

face to face, door to door, residential, small business, retail business, commercial, industrial, corporate or government. The basic principles never change.

If you fully understand something and you practice it until you can do it in your sleep, you will consistently achieve the results you desire, and ultimately, you will achieve any goal you can dream up financially.

Rule: *The Champion always behaves the same way with the customer as they do in the rest of their life. They never have to pretend; they know what to say and do. And they learn this by practicing the art of sales every day.*

When talking with any customer, communicate to them the same way as you do with your friends; naturally, easily and pleasantly. That's how you can do your job every day without stress and with much more success.

Action Items

Partner up with a friend or co-worker and do the following action items together.

1. Pick out a product or service you already sell, or one that you could potentially sell.
2. Take a moment and make up a pitch for it, that you think someone else might use to sell that item. (Creating a simple list of features will be sufficient for this exercise, don't overcomplicate it.)
3. Now, with your partner, speak naturally (like yourself) and sell the product.
4. Repeat the above steps until you feel better about speaking as yourself when selling.
5. Note the results in your journal.

Advice #29
Love What You Are Doing

When you do something you love to do, you will find it's easy to do and takes very little effort. You can't be stopped by anything or anyone when you are doing something you love to do. A fundamental law of success is: the more actions you complete in a workday, the more successful you will be. The more you love your work, the more actions you are willing to complete every day.

Do more, think less. Actions completed lead to success.

Of course, you need knowledge to succeed. But knowledge will come more readily to those who are willing to act, not to those who are sitting around thinking about their problems.

Knowledge will bring nothing to those who are doing nothing. Never try to teach an idler, especially one who claims they never make a mistake. They never make mistakes because they never do anything. Your knowledge will be wasted if you try to share it with someone who is unwilling to take action.

Law of Success:

If you love what you are doing, you will be willing to complete a lot of actions every day. You will do these actions frequently, you will not stop doing these actions, you will be called "lucky" and you will make much more money easily.

Action Items

1. Instead of making a list of all the things you don't like about your company, your product, your co-workers or managers; try this instead: Make a list of all the things you like about your company, your product, your co-workers and managers and owners. Add to this list often. This one action alone can change your entire view of life. (Yes, you can make a list of all the things you like about your friends & family too.)
2. Note the results in your journal.

Advice #30
Ask the Customer for Benefits

Sales is the *service you provide to help the customer make the best choice.* If you just remember this, "selling" is easy.

You could say that "selling" is providing information about the product benefits that can improve the customer's quality of life.

You discuss these positive qualities with the customer, solely in terms of the future use and potential benefit *to the customer*. How will your customer use the product or service to improve their life? The lack of understanding of this important benefit often misleads both customer and salesperson. Why do people buy anything? So they can use it for their benefit!

The customer must win while *using* your product. And your product should work exactly the way you described once they get it home or to the office.

Occasionally a customer comes to you and they only want to "save money," forgetful of how they will use the product. This is why a professional salesperson is needed; to keep the customer from "losing" in the long run! You should never forget the customer's "profit" — *even if the customer forgets*. The customer's "profit" is based on the long-term benefits from using the product: the benefits must be greater than the upfront cost.

Remember this point! You can then create the correct relationship with the customer. Fully understand this, and you will know how to ask the proper questions to get the customer to understand the long-term benefits based on the product's usefulness. Your most important questions lead the customer to understand how and why they are going to use this product, and what short and long-term benefits they can expect from using it. Your skillful questions influence the degree of trust in the future benefits.

Without trust, the sale is impossible.

When you ask your customer what details they are looking for — color, form, function, and so on — you must look for the qualities and benefits the customer forgets, because *you* are the expert in *using* this product, not the customer.

Action Items

1. Pick out a product or service. If you already sell one, pick that one.
2. Create a series of questions you could ask about that product or service, that would lead a prospect to understand how and why they would use that product or service, and what benefits they could expect from using it.
3. Repeat #1 and #2 until you feel comfortable asking questions to lead a prospect to understand a product's benefits.
4. Note the results in your journal.

Part 6: Qualify

> "The essence of your job is: *To help the customer choose the best option... for the* customer!"
> — *Andrey Sizov*

Advice #31
Honor and Respect Your Customer

If you fight with the customer, not allowing them to choose *not* to buy your product, you will become tired, and sooner or later you will cease to love your job.

Rule:

Help your customer by giving them the correct information to make the best choice and allowing them the right <u>not</u> to buy your product, and you won't become tired, you won't strain yourself, you will enjoy working with more people, and best of all, you won't be "fighting" your customers.

By practicing this attitude and doing this consistently, you will become a Sales Champion.

Andrey's First Buying Experience in the United States

During my first trip to the United States, I visited a shoe store in Los Angeles, California. I wasn't going to buy anything. I just wanted to know what style of shoes people wear in America, and I wanted to see how Americans *sell*. I tried on two pairs of shoes, but they didn't fit. I asked for a third pair, with a guilty look, because I didn't want to waste the salesman's time, because I was not going to buy any shoes that day. When the third pair didn't fit me, I hesitantly asked for a fourth pair and the salesman suddenly understood what was happening.

"Are you from Russia?" he asked.

"Yes," I answered.

"Then please wait a second."

The salesman brought someone to translate for us. He then he began to explain, as if taking extra care of Russian customers was part of his normal routine.

"I want to clear something up for you, sir, or I just won't be able to help you. You are the *client* here. You can touch everything and try anything on. If you are still here after closing time, we will wait for you. If you don't want to buy anything, that's really okay. You have the freedom to buy or not to buy. Do you understand, sir? You can visit us and try anything on at any time, and you don't have to buy anything if you don't want to. Please sit back and relax. Our shop is here for you. We can help you, but only if you want us to."

If you have ever taken a tight shoe off, you can understand the relief I experienced after that short speech in my own language. I relaxed. Of course, I did end up buying shoes in that shop. More importantly, I was so impressed with their care for me that I referred many other customers to that shop!

Energy Professionals Perspective

If you show up to work every day with the idea that you are going to close every single energy decision maker you talk to that day, you are setting yourself up to lose.

If you show up to work every day with the idea that you are going to educate energy decision makers on how to bring sustainable energy choices to their company that result in reduced energy costs and more energy independence for their company, you will win. You certainly won't close 100% of the people you talk to, but you will close 100% of the qualified decision makers who really do need your products and services.

It may take several meetings to find out what are the exact "pain points" for that company; what sustainability goals they have; who actually makes the final decision; whether they want to pay a monthly operating expense or make it a capital expense; what is their timeline for installation, etc. You use those meetings to build trust and answer all their questions. Then you present the best solutions based on their needs.

It takes patience and honesty to build long-term relationships.

"My closing rate is 100 percent. I only sell people that want to be sold, and I only recruit people who want to join."
— Xuan Nguyen, Chairman, World System Builders

Advice #32
Always, Always Comfortably Persist

Nothing written here cancels the need for you to *persist* in providing enough information to keep your customer interested in your product or service, create their desire to buy and sign the contract or authorize payment.

As you continue to practice getting customers to truly understand your products benefits, your ability to comfortably persist with every single person will grow. And the percentage of those who buy your product or service will rise higher and higher, while the effort and strain you feel will become less and less. You should always try for 100 percent closing rate — but there is no Sales Champion who can honestly say they close every single person they talk to. They don't worry about closing every single one. This is why the Champion has the highest closing rate, the highest commission, and the biggest smile.

"Never lower your target; increase your actions."
— Grant Cardone

Action Items

1. Think of a time that you did *not* comfortably persist, and you weren't able to make the sale, even though you thought for sure the customer was going to say yes.
2. Notice the point where you stopped caring for that person.
3. Write down how you could have continued to care for that person, and service them and be interested in them. What would the result have been had you done so?
4. Note the results in your journal.

Advice #33
Helping the Customer Choose the Best Option

When we go to buy anything, what do we do? Which words best describe the essence of this process? Usually, it's words like "choose," "look for," "select" or "decide."

If we go to any store, what should we be able to do? We should be able to properly and quickly choose what we need and want. The essence of buying is *choice*. Making the best choice out of a seemingly huge number of options. When we buy something, we have to "choose" something we want or need.

There can be a lot of stress involved in making the right choice. Why do you ask your friends for advice before you buy? They already own the thing you want to buy. What are you going to do with their advice? You are hoping for good information you can *trust* so you can make the right choice, which will be the best choice for you and your situation.

This is exactly what you should always remember when you sell anything.

The essence of your job is: *To help the customer choose the best option for the* customer*!*

It is not always the cheapest option that is the best choice for the customer. The best solution may be the most expensive today but will provide the best benefits for many years to come.

Action Items

1. Think of a time that you let the customer talk you into selling them the cheapest option.
2. Drill with a co-worker how you could have gotten the customer's attention on to the benefits of your product until he realized the best choice is the one that protects him the longest.
3. Note the results in your journal.

Part 7: Educate

> "It's very easy to see that price becomes most important *only* when the customer doesn't see or understand all the benefits. This happens because the sales rep doesn't make sure the customer has seen and understood all the benefits (value). When the value is completely understood by the customer, the price becomes less important in the buying decision."
> — Jim Mathers

Advice #34
Excel in Value

Value consists of the benefits that the customer is *aware* of and *cares* about.

Price will impact the customer's desire to save money.

This is the heart of the purchase process, as well as the sales process. You need to understand this in order to manage this process effectively and not fall victim to the average salesperson's most common complaint: "The customer went with the competitor to get a lower price."

Please note the customer does not purchase based on price alone. They purchase on *perceived profit,* which is the *positive* difference between price and value. A trusted advisor becomes part of the value of the product. Customers will pay more to a trusted advisor because they perceive their trusted advisor as an important part of the long-term value.

It's very easy to see that price becomes most important *only* when the customer doesn't see or understand all the benefits. This happens because the sales rep doesn't *make sure* the customer has seen and understood all the benefits (value). When the value is completely understood by the customer, the price becomes less important in the buying decision.

Your willingness to understand this data is the key factor in your success. Once you truly understand this fact, you will be consistently able to influence the customer's decision in a positive manner. If you don't understand this concept, you will end up arguing about the price, and the customer's attention will go to the competition and their potentially lower price.

Rule: *The customer buys the profit not the price!*

Profit = Value minus Price. The profit is a positive difference between price and value; profit only becomes visible when the sales rep directs the customer's attention to the value. The price is normally obvious to the customer.

The value consists of all the benefits, and there can be a large number of benefits.

The goal of any sales rep is to get the customer talking and discover the factors which can be turned into benefits for that specific customer, and then show as many benefits to the customer as possible.

The ability to handle the customer's unwillingness to look at the benefits of the product or service and to get the customer talking about them, as well as the ability to hold the customer's attention on these things during the whole process of selling, is one of the most important abilities of a sales rep.

You always know if you are doing your job right or not. It's easy for everyone to see:

1. If you ask the customer questions about the benefits of the product or service, and you get the customer talking about how these benefits improve their life, you are doing your job right. You and the customer will be having more fun, and your closing rate will increase as a result.

2. If you find you are arguing with the customer about the price and negative factors of your product or

service, you are not only wasting your valuable time and upsetting potential customers, you are also sabotaging your own success.

Action Items

1. Take a product that you currently sell or are looking to sell. Write down all of its points of value. Include all short-term, mid-term and long-term benefits of that product.
2. Write down the price of that product.
3. Decide for yourself if the value of the product is greater than the price that's being charged for it.
4. Note how this makes you feel in relation to your presentations.
5. Note the results in your journal.

Advice #35
Remember What Motivates People

Logical explanations may get some people to think.

But *emotion* makes people *act*!

How do you create the right emotion to get someone to *act*? Emotions are part of any experience, good or bad. Emotions create the action needed to *avoid something bad* or *acquire something good*.

There is a way to create the right emotions: *you* get the customer to think about certain situations in their life.

How?

Ask them about past situations with negative emotions, and then show how your product will help them avoid similar negative emotions in the future.

Ask about positive situations in the past, and then show how your product can help achieve those positive emotions.

From this we can derive the main competitive advantage of the best sales professionals: *They know that having a lower price or a better product does not guarantee a sale.*

They know that having the ability to *ignite the benefits* in the mind of the customer, creating positive ideas and emotions about their product, guarantees a much, much higher closing rate.

To ignite the benefits, you must find and *practice* ways to smoothly discuss the benefits with the customer not just one time, but many times, asking the customer about their experiences and then always steering them back to the benefits at every opportunity.

How do you use this to the best advantage for both you and the customer? You should be interested in the customer's needs and experiences, find what emotions match those experiences, and continue to ask more questions.

You will find people *love* to talk about themselves, so give them the opportunity to do that. It's easy; just ask them to tell you about their life experiences, especially as related to your product. They will talk about things that are interesting to them. And you will help customers close themselves on your product, *if* you just give them a chance to talk before, during and after you point out the benefits. Don't interrupt them while they are talking!

Action Items

1. Write down a list of things that would get people emotionally involved or emotionally excited about the product or service that you're currently selling.
2. Write down how doing this exercise is going to improve your sales and your ability to deliver more of this product in abundance.
3. Note the results in your journal.

Advice #36
Watch Your Language

One of the traps that unsuccessful sales reps fall into is using *technical* language that confuses the customer. The best sales reps know the exact features and benefits of their products or services. The very best sales reps know the list of positive characteristics and everything that makes up the "value" for the customer, and they always describe these characteristics in words the customer can easily understand.

The customer's language is the language of benefits, advantages and long-term value. The product's language is made up of technical features, with technical words describing those features. Customers tend to get confused by all the technical language used to describe the product. Remember your last trip to a doctor? They use fancy Latin words to tell you what is wrong with you. This normally results in confusion and fear about your condition, which is a very uncomfortable feeling. The result: who likes to go to a doctor?

You are the translator! You are expected to fully understand all the technical product language and turn around and explain those technical features in simple words that show the *benefits* to the customer.

The words "good," "best" or "interesting" will communicate nothing to a customer regarding the value of the product. These general opinions irritate customers and *reduce* their trust in you.

The proper viewpoint: *"How can I help my customer see and fully understand the value and future benefits of this product? How do I become a trusted advisor?"*

The best sales reps fully understand the technical features and how to describe those features in simple terms that show the true value of all the benefits to the customer. This results in a customer who understands what the product or service is going to do to make their life better, and after they sign the contract, the product or service should meet or exceed their expectations.

This is vitally important, and Champions know that this alone is what sets them above their peers.

Champions:
- Do *not* over-promise and under-deliver. They always make every effort to deliver better than expected service.
- Fully understand the value of their product and simply communicate that value to their customer.
- Fully expect their customers to be very satisfied with the product after they get home and use it!
- Fully expect their customer to be able to explain the value they received to others, which results in referral sales.

Energy Professionals Perspective

In learning any new endeavor or field, you will always run across special terminology — words with particular meanings — specific to that field. This is very true of the energy industry. Unless you're experienced in this industry, these words will be foreign to you, just like the words of a language you've never learned would be foreign to you. Imagine traveling to a foreign country and not speaking the language: you would encounter serious difficulty in understanding people with normally simple things like ordering a meal, finding a restroom, or locating a particular point of interest.

Realize that the same is true for your customers and prospects. If they don't understand the terminology of your industry, they'll most likely have the same reaction you would to hearing a foreign language you don't speak: they will feel confused, threatened, or feel that what you're saying is simply "not understandable." This confusion reduces their trust in you. They definitely will NOT understand the VALUE of your product or service.

"The definition of genius is taking the complex and making it simple."
— Albert Einstein

Action Items

1. Write down 5 terms that are specific to your company, product or service, that do not occur in everyday language that your prospect or customer may not understand or relate to.
2. Write down a simple translation for each one of those 5 terms.
3. Note how translating those terms on a regular basis would lead to a greater understanding of your product or service in the mind of your customer.
4. Note the results in your journal.

Advice #37
Build and Maintain a Strong Position with Your Customers

Top sales reps and companies always build and maintain a strong "position" in the minds of their customers. "Positioning" is the idea that distinguishes the company or rep from all the others. Smart companies and reps know exactly what quality distinguishes them from all the rest. They never have to "prove" they are the best. Their attitude reflects supreme confidence in their company, their product and their own ability. This is a very important rule in achieving success and wealth.

To ensure success, you should always be first and foremost in the minds of those who use your products or services.

You should be different from everyone else! That's how you position yourself. You give the customer reasons to remember you above all others. Your attitude, your professionalism, your product knowledge, your *willingness to let the customers talk* about themselves — these all lead to a strong "position" in the customer's mind.

Wealthy and successful sales professionals always know their own value, the value of their company and the value of their products relative to other sales reps and companies. The Champion is always confident about this fact and never tries to prove anything to anybody. "I know who I am, what I'm selling, and I'm proud of my company."

A Champion always makes sure they are representing the best product or service. They confidently lead the customer through all the hurdles to a full understanding of their product or service.

Trying to *prove* or *persuade* equals "justifying some hidden weakness" to a customer. And this is an indicator of a poor salesperson.

Action Item

Write down all the ways that you, your product and your company are better than your competition.

Advice #38
Why Salespeople Stop Liking Their Products

During our case studies, we consistently observed the following action:

At the end of the proposal or pitch, the sales rep asks the customer if they are going to buy the product. If the customer says "no," the rep tends to ask the customer what they *don't* like about the product. Instantly, all the customer's attention goes on the drawbacks, not the advantages.

Sales rep: *"Will that be cash or credit?"*
Customer: *"We're going to look for something else. This isn't exactly what we wanted."*
Sales rep: *"What didn't you like?"*

And they start talking about "what the customer didn't like."
Size, shape, color, price, etc.

What happens?

If only 2 out of 10 customers were closed — and unfortunately this is the average around the world — the sales rep has "listened" to 80 percent of the prospects complaining about the product's drawbacks. By the end of each day, the sales rep becomes totally convinced that there are many more drawbacks to their product than advantages. In other words, the customer has "sold" the sales rep, instead of the other way around.

Unless *you* want to be convinced by your prospects all day, every day, that your product or service is not worth paying for, *you* must change something immediately!

First, make sure you fully understand all the advantages of your product or service (value). If you have honestly found out everything about what you are being paid to sell, and you realize you would not buy this product or service for your own family or friends, then go find a better product, service or company to work with.

If you realize after close observation that your product or service is truly valuable for people you actually care about, then study all the reasons why you should sell your product or service and memorize those benefits! True Champions never sell anything they don't believe in.

Quit asking what they didn't like or why they didn't buy. Remember, the customer always has the right "to buy or not to buy." You have the right to find out what the customer *did* like about your product!

Start asking questions about what they like about your product. Also remind them about all the attributes of your product and get them telling you the effect those attributes will have on their life.

Action Items

1. Pick a product or service that you currently sell.
2. List out each and every advantage and benefit of that product.
3. Decide that these are of benefit and of value to your customer.
4. With a fresh perspective of looking at these benefits of your product or service, note how you feel about your product or service now.
5. Note the results in your journal.

Advice #39
Love What You Have, and Be Willing to Share with Others

Wealthy people always have things they enjoy, things that bring them pleasure. And normally, they are willing to share the things they enjoy. They have beautiful houses and throw big parties to share their wealth with their friends. They have nice cars and boats and invite their friends to enjoy them as well. They have planes and invite their friends to fly with them.

Poor people always have things they *don't* like, things they love to complain about. The things they do like always seem to belong to someone else. They are always looking *over there*, never enjoying what they actually own. It doesn't mean they have no money — it just means they have a "poor" attitude toward life and material objects.

The viewpoint of a wealthy person: *"I enjoy what I have, and I'm always willing to share."*

The viewpoint of a poor person: *"I don't have anything I like, I wish I had what they have."*

Wealthy thought: *"I always have something valuable."*

Poor thought: *"I never have anything valuable."*

Hence the rule of success: *Always love what you have and be willing to share with others. For a Champion, it's a guiding rule. Champions focus on the positive in everything they do and have, and they are constantly trying to share this positive attitude with everyone they meet.*

Action Items

1. Honestly look at your own attitude toward your life right now.
2. Then, write down the things you enjoy about you, and the things that you think are valuable in your life; this may include your skills, your friends and family.
3. Decide that you are willing to share these things with others.
4. Note down how that makes you feel.
5. Record the results in your journal.

Advice #40
Before You Take, You Must Give

Everybody gives something to the people around them: words, thoughts, actions, looks and emotions. These can be perceived by anyone. A definite trace of this "gift" stays with a customer after you talk with them.

The secret is: people always give something they consider they have a large amount of. People give to others what they believe they are "rich" in, something they have naturally accumulated their whole life.

If you accumulate joy, then you will give out joy. If you accumulate a lot of kindness and love toward people, you will leave kindness and love behind with everyone you talk to.

If you accumulate spite or fear, then you will hand out spite and fear to everyone you meet. People who are chronically afraid leave fear behind them.

If you are full of respect toward yourself, then it is much easier to give respect and support to others. If you don't appreciate yourself, it is much harder to appreciate others.

A true winner treats others as winners.

In sales, this mechanism displays itself very clearly because the following law is always in play:

Before you take, you must give.

And what do the best sales reps normally give? Something they think will have *value* when it is given. That's why it's very important for a sales rep to think well of themselves, their product and their company. Anyone can change how they think about themselves, their product and their company, if they really want to.

What "gift" are you giving your customers? It may take some work and practice to improve your gift, but aren't *you* worth it?

Is achieving your goals worth your effort and dedication to improve the way you think about yourself, your product and your company?

When you are confident in yourself, your customers can see that. And, when they can see you truly believe in your product, and you genuinely want to assist them in choosing the product and living life better for it, you move from being "someone who wants to sell something" to a "trusted advisor." When you deliver a product worth having, you get more referrals and repeat sales.

Action Item

Answer this question: Besides simply your product or service, what else do you give your prospects that is valuable? Note the answer for yourself, and in your journal.

Advice #41
Practice the Two Main Qualities

There are two main qualities or skills a professional sales rep must have as a foundation and the rest of the necessary skills will naturally follow them.

1. *Total certainty* of the ability to do one's job under any circumstances, with any customer, in any situation, no matter how uncomfortable.

If you already have this quality, then everything else you learn in this book will help you become a very wealthy Sales Champion.

If you don't have this quality already, don't give up. You can acquire this quality by practicing the advices of this book every day, until you notice that all of a sudden, you *do* have total certainty of your ability.

2. The willingness and skill to find solutions that really work for different situations, knowing and using the fundamental rules.

The fundamental rules of professional sales are in this book.

It's impossible to give you specific advice for every single situation you could run into in your career. There are an unlimited number of completely different situations you could face. Our purpose is to teach you to find your own words, your own pitch, and your own solutions to handle any situation you run into. If your willingness to find solutions is based on the proper *fundamental rules*, you will be very successful, stress-free, super confident and very highly paid.

Champions become Champions because they understand and apply the basic fundamental rules to their profession.

Champions aren't just born that way. They study, practice and learn to be Champions. So can you.

"I don't know if I practiced more than anybody, but I sure practiced enough. I still wonder if somebody — somewhere — was practicing more than me."
— *Larry Bird*

Action Items

1. Write down 3 things that you could practice on today that would help you improve your total certainty and increase your willingness and skill to find solutions that really work.
2. If you're in charge of a team, write down 3 things that your team could benefit from practicing to increase their certainty.
3. Work out a regular time during your week to increase your skillset, and the skillset of your team.
4. Note and track the results in your journal.

Advice #42
Don't Drive the Customer Away

There is a tendency to pressure and overload a customer with information, which results in the customer becoming less interested in the salesperson and the product. The customer gets confused and overwhelmed, and then walks away.

Is the customer listening to you?

You must always be observing the customer. Your success depends on knowing what's going on in the customer's mind — where their attention is, what they're thinking about.

You don't need to read minds or make wild guesses. Look and observe! Listen carefully. You can tell if the customer is listening to you or not. You can tell if they are smiling, frowning or bored. Don't be so interested in your own pitch that you stop being interested in what is happening with the customer. This applies to phone as well as face to face sales! Listen carefully. Does their voice change? Do they put you on hold for several minutes? You can observe carefully if you practice. You can look and listen for details that tell you the customer is getting bored or frustrated with your presentation.

This seems too obvious to some people but go home or to a friend's house tonight and watch a few conversations. Watch the person speaking and the person "listening." Is the one talking even looking at the other? Can you tell when the person being talked "at" loses interest? This is not a hard skill to learn. But you must be willing to practice *looking*!

It may amaze you to see something you never noticed before. You can always tell when the other person loses interest in your conversation. The trick is to notice it instantly and then do something about it. Ask a question to find out more information and get back on track. Don't waste your time or the customer's by talking on and on past the point the customer stopped listening to you.

The main idea is to control their level of interest and to make sure that they are listening to you by observing their reactions while you talk. You find out what they are interested in by asking good questions and then give them the information they are interested in.

If you know your product, have done your homework and researched the customer — or asked enough questions to find out what the customer is looking for — you now know the customer's concerns and interests. Just start giving them easily understandable information on how they can handle their problem using your product or service.

If you didn't do any research or ask any questions about what they need, you have to be very attentive. Most importantly, watch their eyes. If they look away, even for a second, you should stop immediately and ask, "Did you think of something?" Same thing if they stop listening on the phone, ask more questions on the phone and get them talking. Listen carefully to what they say, they will give you clues as to what is important to them.

Ask for details: "What do you think about this?" This is worth doing every time you suspect that you've lost their attention. Don't be afraid to make a mistake. It never hurts to ask what the customer is thinking about — they will tell you. Especially on a phone call. If you feel the customer drifting away, do not just talk faster and louder! That doesn't work.

You should be aware of the customer's attention, because if you miss that moment, you will lose the customer. If this occurs and you don't notice, then you are talking *at* them, not with them, and this will work against you. The result? The customer makes a decision: *"It's time to go, and I have to find a good reason to get out of here. I hope this salesperson stops talking soon, because I'm not listening to them."* They will look around for any excuse to leave and listen for you to say something they disagree with so they can leave quickly.

The error is: *not paying attention to the customer's reactions while you are talking, and then continuing to load them with more information after that moment when the customer indicated they were no longer interested.*

Sales reps tend to talk too much. Ask questions to get the *customer* talking!

Learn to keep your eyes on the customer while you are talking. The moment you notice the slightest indicator of the loss of attention or interest, you should ask them what they are thinking about, and get them to tell you.

If you are on the phone, listen carefully. Listen for changes in their emotional tone and listen to background noises. On the phone you can't look, but you sure can listen. Get the customer talking. If you ask enough questions and give them the exact information they need to solve their problems, the customer will close themselves.

The best way to know what someone else is thinking is to simply ask them enough questions to find out.

"Confusion equals 'no.'"
— Wes Faria

Action Items

1. Go somewhere — your own home, a friend's house, or another location where people are talking — and observe others in conversation. Carefully note when the person being talked to loses interest, even slightly.
2. Practice yourself talking to others and being able to see when the other person "tunes out" even just a little. Ask them what's happening, or what they just thought of. Get them back in the conversation.
3. Do the above 2 steps until you can comfortably spot when someone has "left" the conversation, and you can bring them back again.
4. Note the results in your journal.

Advice #43
Help the Customer Make the Best Choice

The art of sales is all about helping the customer obtain the necessary information to make the best choice.

Let's break down this process systematically. What does this service to the customer consist of?

- What information do you have at your fingertips that will help your client make the best and most logical decision?
- What are the priorities or needs that the client has that would make this a valuable product or service for them?
- Do you have a clear understanding of the value beyond simply "saving money" that can be communicated to the client?
- What is the way for you to be able to accept payment once the client has made the decision to move forward?

The main function of a sales rep is to help the customer get through the steps above. This is what we expect from a professional sales rep. Both your company and the customer are expecting this service.

You can use the following phrase: *"Let me show you some of the benefits of this particular product or service that might be of interest to you. Then we'll both work out the most important benefit for your situation, and I'll do my best to help you make the best decision for you."*

"First be best, then be first."
— Grant Tinker

Advice #44
The Four Things You *Should* Talk About

Professional sales is the art of increasing the customer's knowledge about the product's benefits, and enhancing the long-term value of the product from the customer's viewpoint. As a result, you receive fair payment from the customer in a timely manner.

Please note that the payment should result from the customer's willingness to take advantage of your offer — not to escape your "high-pressure" tactics. They should give you their money with pleasure. They will return to you and do it again and again, *and* they will refer their friends.

You will have a much higher closing percentage when you show your customer the advantages of four things:

1. *You and your company.*

2. Your product information and knowledge of benefits and ability to communicate this effectively and increase the customer's certainty in making this decision.

3. The product itself as a solution for the customer's long-term problems.

4. More information about the background of your company to increase the comfort and trust factor with your prospect.

If you do a great job of explaining all four points above so the customer really understands but still doesn't buy right now, you still "win" and you have done your job, fully educating the customer on the best value for them. By focusing on giving the customer a perfect sales experience, your overall closing efficiency will continue to rise.

But if you don't understand what a "win" actually is, and you assign yourself a "failure" too often, you can't help but feel like you're "losing." You will stop selling and will become extremely stressed.

It's not difficult for a winner to let a customer walk away without buying something. The winner just continues to repeat the successful actions as often as necessary, without worry, without stress or strain, to many, many prospects, and this will result in a higher and higher closing rate.

Action Items

1. Fully understand, for yourself, items 1 - 4 for anything you sell, or want to sell.
2. Practice describing the advantages of points 1 - 4, until you feel comfortable doing it.
3. Note the results in your journal.

Advice #45
Always Think of the Future

The role of a salesperson is to help create steady growth and prosperity of their company. New prospects, recommended by existing customers, are one of the main indicators of the success and prosperity of your sales team and your company. While there are also potential customers who find out about your product or service but don't buy anything yet, they *will* come back and buy, depending on how well the sales professionals do their job.

What does any customer want from a salesperson?

Well, what do *you* want when *you* are buying something as a customer? How do you want to be treated during the sales process when you are trying to buy something?

You want your problem solved the best way for you, right? Not just the cheapest product or service, but the best value for your long-term future. You might want to be comfortable talking to the salesperson, not feeling forced into a decision you aren't sure of. You probably want them to respect your power of choice and give you enough information to make a "smart" decision, not the "cheapest" decision.

How do you feel as a customer when a salesperson fails to tell you about all the options, even if they are more expensive? How do you feel about the salesperson when you get home and find out you saved some money, but the quality is nowhere near what you thought it would be?

Don't fall into the trap of "cheaper is always better." It is not true and does not lead to long-term customer satisfaction.

Energy Professionals Perspective

This point cannot be overstated: to work in the energy industry, you really have to envision a long-term relationship with the people and companies that you serve. Your view of the future — seeing how you can serve those customers long-term — is going to differentiate you from everyone else in the industry.

Action Items

1. Envision all the different ways that you can build a long-term relationship with your client.
2. Select 5 of your clients that you can see yourself having long-term relationships with. List out the services that you're going to provide to them now and into the future.
3. Note the results in your journal and keep track of these 5 clients and how you are doing week to week with them.

Advice #46
Getting Customers to Fully Understand Value

"Customers know everything about the product already. They are not interested in more information. They only want the lowest price!"

Sales reps say this to their managers all the time, all over the world, in many different languages. It's a great excuse for not closing customers.

The only way the customer will understand your value is if you take the time to ask enough questions and show the long-term benefits that match what the customer is really looking for. Sometimes customers do not know what they are immediately looking for! Asking the right questions and even more importantly, letting the customer answer without cutting them off with your "sales" pitch, will result in the customer being willing to listen to the benefits that fully handle their problem. Then the customer will perceive the long-term value.

The truth is that people love to learn more about the things they are interested in. This is often hidden because they may feel bad that they don't already know, and they are in no hurry to display their lack of understanding.

They appreciate professional sales reps who care enough to take the time to teach them, and they will refer their friends to these professionals over and over again. By getting the customer to fully understand your product's benefits, or how it solves problems related to them, you immediately make the customer your friend.

One of the most common customer complaints is sales rep

incompetence. In defense of such complaints, sales reps assert that they *do* know what they're talking about. The problem is that if *you* understand, but the customer *doesn't* understand, the customer is going to say that *you* are incompetent.

Therefore, you must take the time to ask the prospect questions and discover exactly where their interest lies and exactly what their problems are. Then, relate your product details that connect with their interest and solve their problems until they *do* understand. When the customer learns something new, they'll give you all the credit for informing them about it.

This is exactly how you create free promotion for yourself. People love to talk about things they understand. Customers who really learn from you will tell others to come see you.

Even if they don't pay you right now, you've made them into an ally. Get them to understand something fully and it will pay dividends to you for a long time to come.

Energy Professionals Perspective

One of the concepts that helped me early on in my career was the fact that in the energy industry, you have to be sitting "on the same side of the table" as the customer. If you can easily take the customer's viewpoint, and look at the problem through their eyes, you can find the best solutions faster as their consultant.

Many times, energy sales reps assume a scenario of "me versus the customer." You automatically overcome the war between sales and customers if you are sitting on the same side as the customer, helping the customer to choose the best product or service for their specific situation.

Changing this point of view of sitting across from or opposing the customer, to sitting on the same side as and helping the customer, will help you to increase your sales now and well into the future. The proof of this will be your rising number of referral sales from very satisfied customers who trust you as their energy advisor.

And never be afraid to ask your customer for a referral. When you do a great job of solving your customer's problems, you make them look good, and they really want to do something to help you. When they find out that giving you one of their friends will help you out, they will gladly refer. Don't assume anything. Just ask for the referral and you will be surprised! Remember, you will only get those referrals if you do a great job of helping the customer understand the full value of your service.

Action Items

1. Write down 10 questions you can ask your customer to get them talking about what problems they are trying to solve, what long term benefits they are looking for, what experiences they have had had in the past, good or bad.
2. Select 5 of your prospects that you can call and ask more questions to get them talking and be aware of how well you listen and note down what they need.
3. Note the results in your journal after you call them.

Advice #47
Fall in Love with Your Product

What does a great sales rep do? They gradually, step by step, communicate the value of their proposition to the customer. They display the appropriate benefits of the product and get the customer to fully understand that the value of your product is far greater than the cost.

But is it very clear to you that *you* really need to believe in the value of your proposition first? To communicate effectively, *you* should believe in what you are selling!

YOU SHOULD FALL IN LOVE WITH YOUR PRODUCT AND YOUR COMPANY IN ORDER TO BE WILDLY SUCCESSFUL.

Every time a customer has experienced dealing with a sales rep who is truly passionate about their company and product, they walk away imbued with a portion of that passion.

If the value of a product grows in the customer's mind after the sales rep contacts them, it means the sales rep did their job correctly.

Rule: *You either increase or decrease the value of your product in the customer's mind while you talk to them. The more you love your company and product, the more likely you are to increase the value and increase the prospect's willingness to deal with your company in the future.*

Best of all, you will find that this customer will communicate your passion to their friends and family, increasing your commission with less effort on your part.

Understand this: if you can't find a reason to be passionate about your product, service or your company, then you will find it impossible to be passionate about your day to day activities.

There are only two main courses of action if you really want to be a Champion.

1. Change your mind. If your company is successfully selling a good product or service and many customers are happy with your company, then it is up to you to change your attitude and find several reasons to be passionate about your company. It is possible to create passion in your life. You picked this book up for a reason. If you intended to be an average person, doing an average job and having an average life, then you would never be looking for ways to improve yourself. This book is based on the lessons learned by two very successful sales leaders, each with over 30 years of sales experience. This book is intended to create new sales leaders in the world. Great sales reps are made, they are not born.

2. Find a different company. If your company is not honestly providing high quality products and service, and if your company does not treat customers or employees fairly, then leave. It is impossible to be passionate about serving your customers if you are always afraid they will come looking for you because they feel ripped off or lied to. It's impossible to ask for referrals when you know the customer may be angry when they find out you were not telling the whole truth. This may be hard to swallow, difficult to confront. It's your life. You decide where you work. You decide how well you will be paid. You decide whether or not you will be passionate about your work. It's up to you.

Make a decision. Choose a new path if you need to.

Change your attitude if the company is actually doing a great job with customers.

Decide!

Don't just sit back and complain about your company and your products.

Get the facts and make a decision.

You are not a slave.

We hope you will decide to be a Champion.

Action Items

1. Write down all of the ways that you could be in love with your product or service.
2. Write down all of the ways that you could be in love with your company.
3. With fresh perspective, write down how you feel about your product and company now.
4. If you can't find anything to love about your product or your company, then be honest with yourself.
5. Note the results in your journal.

Part 8: Agreement

> "The main goal in sales is to help people create *positive feelings* regarding the products they are looking to buy. This is a huge addition to the material benefit of the purchase and is very often worth more than money. The product sitting there silently, or its price tag, can't create these positive emotions. Advertising on the internet will try to do this, and can help to start the process, but it can only actually be done by a good sales rep asking the right questions and *listening* to the customer!"
> — Jim Mathers

Advice #48
Don't Create a "Battle" Scenario

If a sales rep doesn't honor the customer's right to choose — "to buy or not to buy" — they automatically walk into a fight. What fight? It becomes a "war." No punches are thrown, but the customer is fighting for their freedom to choose, and the sales rep fights *against* that freedom. Whether the sales rep understands it's a battle or not, they become tired of fighting. Why? It's not easy to fight all the time! As a result, the work becomes serious, hard and eventually unbearable.

It's really very simple:

"Please, come in and look at what we have to offer. If you see something you like, we will be very happy to help you. Don't buy anything you don't need. There's no rush — we don't want you to make the wrong choice. A wrong choice is more expensive for our company. And to help you make the best choice for you, we have professionals whose main purpose is to save you from buying things you don't need. They are happy to do their job."

The phrases vary but the main idea is always exactly the same. Anyone can be trained to do this. You just direct the attention of your managers, consultants and sales professionals to this main point of servicing the customer's needs first. It has been proven time and again that more money, customers and pleasure come as a result in those companies where this is done correctly.

Energy Professionals Perspective

In the energy industry we are dealing with multi-million-dollar decisions that affect the bottom-line profits of our commercial and industrial customers. We train our consultants to ask as many questions as needed to really find out the full solutions available for that particular customer. This is not a sales gimmick. We can't provide the best service if we don't take the time to find out all the details and problems our client is facing in their hotel chain, manufacturing plant, school or hospital.

By patiently analyzing the customer's needs, we wind up selling on the "same side of the table" as they are, and we help them select the best energy solutions for their company, not our company.

Advice #49
Learn Why People Really Buy

People do not buy goods or services. They do not buy "things."

People buy because of their *emotions*. They buy based on what they "feel" about the product or service. They feel "bad" or "good" and that results in either a sale or just walking away. And this emotion is created out of the discussion of the benefits, which they can fully understand, and in turn they share these benefits with others, which results in "referral sales."

Whoever shows the most benefits wins!

Rule: The real secret of product benefits is that the <u>same</u> benefit acts as a *new* and *separate* benefit *every time* it is brought to the customer's attention!

The customer's interest in the product increases every time the sales rep *or* the customer talks about any particular benefit. Each time a benefit is brought up in conversation, it increases the positive emotion and willingness of the customer to buy your product, because they really start to understand the value to them.

The main goal in sales is to help people create *positive feelings* regarding the products they are looking to buy. This is a huge addition to the material benefit of the purchase and is very often worth more than money. The product sitting there silently, or its price tag, can't create these positive emotions. Advertising on the internet will try to do this, and can help to start the process, but it can only actually be done by a good sales rep asking the right questions and *listening* to the customer!

Energy Professionals Perspective

There can be overwhelming lists of benefits and marketing materials applauding the various features of everything from complex pricing contracts to onsite generation to solar power with battery backups. An amateur mistake is feeling that you have to go through *all* of the product benefits of your company in order to have a successful sale.

The real sales professional will get the most agreement from finding a specific product benefit that suits a specific client need and matching the benefit and the need together. This will make for a very positive sales experience.

Make sure that you don't overwhelm a prospect with *all* of the benefits all at once. Help to instill positive feelings with a precise set of benefits that your product or service has to offer, and again this comes from asking the right questions, listening carefully to the client, knowing your product well and being able to match up your product features with what your client actually needs and wants.

The other point to understand specifically for energy consultants is that there may be several major problem areas. Take the time to do a full assessment of where the most energy is being wasted, where the most money can be saved with minimal investment and put all the information you have gathered into an energy strategy that the client can easily understand.

A competent energy professional can help commercial & industrial customers control and reduce their energy spend with lower electricity and natural gas prices, demand response programs, onsite solar & wind power supply, backup battery solutions, onsite natural gas generators, energy intelligence software & monitoring, HVAC refurbishment and Smart LED lighting solutions to name just a few. Strategic energy consulting becomes a vital service to sort through the apparent confusion and help the customer choose the best options for their organization.

Action Items

1. Make a list of several benefits that your product or service offers.
2. List out the emotions that those solutions would give to your clients, should you be able to help them solve a problem.
3. Note the results in your journal.

Advice #50
Raise Your Sales Efficiency

Different sales reps have different levels of efficiency based on their closing effectiveness. These figures are based on the closing success of various types of sales reps. They are used to highlight the difference between an average sales rep and a Champion.

The lowest level of efficiency
This type of sales rep tells the customer about all the benefits, barely stopping to take a breath, like a locomotive chugging down the track, making as few stops as possible and never allowing the customer to talk. This level of efficiency equals 10 percent, and obviously, it's just not very effective. Most customers will hardly ever give you the opportunity to talk that much. Unfortunately, this is the level of the average sales rep in the world.

The next level of efficiency
This next level is 50 percent efficient. This occurs when a sales rep asks questions about the customer's needs and past experiences and *listens* to the answers.

By listening, you sell. It is much more difficult than talking, because it "seems" that you can't sell if you don't talk. But listening is exactly the action that sells. Of course, you have to ask questions, but direct the questions at the discussion of problems, which can be solved using your product. After you ask, you should listen and listen carefully, *then* ask more questions. At this stage each question, asked properly, hits the mark. Each question brings the customer more understanding of your product and service. Result: 50 percent effective, or 5 times more effective than the average sales rep.

The highest level of efficiency
This level occurs when a sales rep *creates* the customer's *willingness* to talk about advantages of the product or service for themselves, and then the customer finds out for themselves that the product or service is really useful for them.

If a person is interested in something, they will talk about it. So, get your customer telling *you* about the advantages, and they sell themselves. Here is where the knowledge of the customer based on research pays off. Keeping every appointment on time perfectly. Asking the right question every time. Steering the customer's attention to his problems and his goals and then showing your products' benefits and how they solve the problem or help achieve the goal. Result: 100 percent effective! This is the level of the Champion.

"The mental toughness process is not about getting from good to very good — it's about getting from good to great. Anyone who settles for very good is destined to spend their golden years bathed in a sea of regret, wondering why."
— *Steve Siebold*

Action Items

1. Find a mentor or someone who is successful within your company or industry, preferably someone familiar with your track record as a salesperson.
2. Go over and review this chapter with them.
3. Discuss with your mentor your level of efficiency and be honest with yourself. Together come up with some potential ways to increase your efficiency so that you can actually be much better at servicing your client base.
4. List out specific action items that you're going to take as a result of this meeting in order to be able to raise your efficiency and get closer to the highest level.
5. Read the book Relentless by Tim Grover.
6. Look for other books related to your industry. You can only become a Champion by knowing more than the best sales reps in your industry.
7. Note and track the results in your journal.

Advice #51
Don't Just Talk About Advantages — Demonstrate Them

Demonstration is very important for the sales process and getting the customer to truly understand how your product or service will benefit them. Don't just talk about the advantages — show them.

If you sell face-to-face, it's easy: you just give the product to your customer and show how it works. But what do you do if you sell on the phone, or if you sell a service that can't be handled like an object? It can still be demonstrated! You may have to use your imagination, but it can be done, and it makes your job much easier.

If it's a service, tell them how it is usually delivered, saving some of the benefits to show and demonstrate later. Take the installation of windows as an example; your customer worries about damage to their house. You can show what actions are taken to protect the house during installation. You can provide letters from customers who specifically stated that no damage was done during their installation, and how they benefited from their new windows.

Another very effective method is to tell a story about how this advantage is being implemented, or about how this product is being manufactured. While selling anything from shoes to furniture, the best sales reps tell stories about the manufacturing process, the care taken, where the manufacturer is located, and so on, in order to show how the important aspects were implemented. *Stories* are often used very successfully for creating emotional impact and demonstrating benefits for customers. Especially on the phone and not face to face, where you can't just show the product. Your stories of other customers' past experiences can create a visual and emotional picture in the customer's mind that he won't forget. If it's a great story, he will tell others the same story, and that leads to more referral sales.

Energy Professionals Perspective

In the energy industry, we're dealing with natural gas market changes that can change instantly based on a multitude of factors. These market swings can make a commodity procurement contract invalid before the customer gets a chance to sign the contract. Larger contracts for onsite generation, solar power projects, roof repairs, Demand Response programs, battery backups and micro-grid applications can be somewhat complicated and hard to demonstrate easily.

There are two fundamental ways that we demonstrate things in the energy industry:

- Case studies. There are literally dozens of existing case studies with full financial analyses and drawings which demonstrate successful applications. Have a couple for each type of project that you are going to be selling. Using a power point type of presentation puts this clearly in front of the customer, and you can do this type of demonstration over a conference call.
- Customer success stories illustrating specific problems or goals that your service or product handled.

For example, about a year ago, one of our own Champions came across a church that one of the junior advisors was trying to help. The church administrator thought they already had a great price for their electricity. But the Champion persisted kindly and offered to do a free bill analysis for the church. It turned out that the church was on a variable contract that was not tied to any market index and the month that we evaluated, they were being charged 27 cents/kwh for just the commodity! Our Champion explained what that meant and how much it was costing them per year. He got them protected by a 3-year fixed commodity price under 7 cents/kwh. That saved the church about $25,000 per year. This story is used by other energy advisors to point out potential problems and the resultant value of a utility bill audit.

Action Items

1. For any product or service that you sell, figure out some of the features and how you can demonstrate them to a prospect. Note the results in your journal.
2. Work with marketing to create a presentation that you can email to customers to demonstrate the most important parts of your product and service. Practice giving this demonstration to people over the phone or face to face.
3. Have 2 or 3 stories of your own experience with past customers or ask the best sales reps to share some of their stories with you. Practice telling each story until you know them cold and when to use which story.

Advice #52
Never Sell Second-Rate

Why is saving money more important for some people than high quality? You may observe that many people will settle for less quality in the hope of saving some money. For some reason, many people will buy something that is not exactly what they really want, but it saves them money.

We call this phenomenon a "second-rate" purchase. For some reason, either to save money or because someone else said it was good enough, people settle for less.

Check it out yourself. Look in your closet and count how many pieces of clothing are hanging up that you never wear. "Second-rate" has a certain quality: *you don't really use it, but you can't seem to throw it away either*. It just hangs there, upsetting you from time to time. "Why did I buy that?"

Don't buy things you don't really like, even if they're on sale! A great sales rep is like "first-aid" in such cases. Learn how to show your customer the value of higher quality items and show how expensive "second-rate" items will be for them at the end of the day.

Don't be afraid to ask the question: "Why would you waste your money to buy problems for yourself?" or "Why would you buy something that isn't what you really want?" or "How expensive is it if you buy it and never use it?" or "How much money did you really save, if you never use it?"

Energy Professionals Perspective

Many of the products and services available in the energy industry appear very similar to each other. There can be various factors which cause people to prefer one company or product over another. These factors can be as simple as industry rating, marketing, branding, reputation or a more effective sales force.

One of the best things you can do is add value to the relationship by being an excellent consultant and take the time to follow-up. By your successful actions alone, you add that higher quality service that makes two similar brands appear quite different.

Just by making yourself an indispensable ally in your customer's search for energy-related solutions, you will create an unforgettable and high-quality experience for that client.

Be indispensable.

Action Items

1. Have you ever had the experience of spending a little less on a cheaper product, getting it home, and wishing you'd just bought the better product? Remember what that was like. (NOTE: You can always ask your customer the same question, if they're looking to "save money.")
2. Make sure that you are absolutely certain as to why your product or service is the best, and totally worth the money. Review features and benefits, and successes that customers have recently had.
3. Drill with a team member handling them on the above, until you can do so smoothly.
4. Note the results in your journal.

Advice #53
Appreciate What the Customer Gives to You

You should understand and respect the *stress* your customer is under during the sales process, especially at the very beginning and at the very end. Making decisions is not always easy, and any actual purchase requires a decision be made right now. Customers usually don't even understand what they are experiencing. When the sales rep understands and appreciates what the customer is going through, this understanding is often the *most significant* contribution to the customer's decision to buy at that moment.

The customer expects to get *valuable information in exchange for their time and attention.* If the sales rep does not provide this valuable information, they may get the idea that they just "stole" the customer's time and attention. The salesperson may start to feel uncomfortable because they are not keeping up their end of the basic exchange, and they become unwilling to continue talking to their customer.

If you continue to offer the customer very useful information, they will easily maintain their willingness to talk with you. If you provide clear and necessary information (not just meaningless fluff), and if the customer understands the value of this information, then you will feel no discomfort, and you will both enjoy the time you spend talking with each other, whether the customer chooses to buy something right now or not.

Rule: *Stop wasting your customer's time and attention by chattering nonsense, throwing worn-out sales phrases and "closing" patter at them. The customer gives you their* *attention and time, and they expect to receive something valuable in exchange. Your information is valuable when it actually serves the customer's needs.*

Action Items

1. Determine for yourself how valuable the customer's time, attention and point of view are to you.
2. Make a list of the knowledge that you have that would provide value to the customer, in exchange for their time, attention and point of view.
3. List out all the ways that you can appreciate the client's time, attention and point of view.
4. Note the results in your journal.

Advice #54
Learn Not to Make These 2 Fatal Mistakes

People remember and return again to those sales professionals who:

- Treat the customer with respect and educate them to make the best choice versus forcing them to buy.
- Don't recommend a product if they realize it doesn't really fit the customer's needs.
- Get the customer to understand that a more expensive product that is of higher long-term quality *actually is* the better option for the customer.
- Give additional valuable information about their product or service; for example, they show the customer how to use all the benefits of the product and give them a follow-up call to make sure they are satisfied.

We can easily remember salespeople like this. In fact, there is a fairly common way to find sales reps that fit this mold — we simply ask our friends and family, "Where did you buy your cell phone? Do you trust them? Did you get a good deal?" Remember, a "good deal" does not always mean the lowest price.

The *first* mistake would be to sell your customer something they don't really need or that doesn't fully solve their problem. This mistake causes most of the "returned" items and commission chargebacks. Avoid this mistake and your chargebacks will disappear.

The *second* mistake is the one that separates the average sales rep from the Champion. When the sales rep knows the customer needs a higher quality and more expensive solution to create a long-term benefit but doesn't take the time and energy to really get the customer to understand the full situation, they are letting that customer down.

Champions persist. They're willing to communicate enough, take enough action and have enough courage to get the customer to understand the truth of long-term quality and value. Champions have high referral rates and customers that continually come back to purchase other items or services.

Champions also consistently get customers to understand and pay extra for high quality products and services. This is exactly why Champions make a *lot* more money than the average sales rep.

Action Items

1. Select a product that would be of need to your customers.
2. Select one prospect from your list who you are preparing to present to, or to whom you have presented in the past.
3. Write down all of the ways that your product or service would solve a problem for that particular prospect.
4. Look at all of the ways that your product, service or company provides high quality to the prospect regardless of cost.
5. Write down some factors from #4 that you will bring up or could have brought up to a past prospect.
6. Note the results in your journal.

Advice #55
Don't Prevent Your Own Sales

Here is a common complaint from sales reps: "I spend the time to educate the customer, and then they go and buy it somewhere else for less."

According to actual experience, people tend to go to places where they feel good. A person will come back to the same place over and over. This rule is not canceled by low or high prices. This rule does not submit to the laws of logic. Emotions have their *own* laws!

The atmosphere of a place where you felt good will draw you back. You go there even if logic tells you that you can save money elsewhere.

This is where the false idea of having to "pressure" people by arguing with them comes into play. This idea assumes that you are in a "fight" with the customer. This is the "war" between the customer and the salesperson.

Argument is a reason or set of reasons that you use to persuade others that they are wrong, and you are right. This position assumes there is a fight, and that one person will win, and one person will lose.

The truth is, that the *sale is a very emotional thing* from start to finish, but it doesn't have to be a war.

People don't buy goods and services. They buy:

- **Emotions**
- **Thoughts**
- **Imagination**
- **Feelings**

- **Expectations**
- **Anticipated rewards**

Customers will pay their hard-earned money for these valuable ideals.

Don't lose this advantage for your company and yourself. Sometimes businesses without commissioned salespeople appear more attractive to the average customer. But a business like this normally attracts less competent salespeople from other companies. A professional salesperson is a significant advantage for any company. This is a fact.

Sales professionals know that customers buy on emotion much more often than logic. They buy because they are afraid to lose something. They pay more in some places because they like the way they are treated. They buy because they fully understand and feel safe in their decision that their long-term goals will be met.

The professional uses *all* these feelings combined with excellent product knowledge to make it safe for the customer to *buy now*.

"*Imagination is more important than knowledge. For knowledge is limited, whereas imagination embraces the entire world, stimulating progress, giving birth to evolution.*"
— Albert Einstein

Action Items

1. Write down some of the emotions, thoughts, imagination, feelings, expectations and anticipated rewards that your clients will get from the products and services that you're representing.
2. Write down some of the emotions, thoughts, imagination, feelings, expectations and anticipated rewards that clients would expect from being in business with you.
3. Decide that you can deliver those emotions, thoughts, imagination, feelings, expectations and anticipated rewards — and start delivering them in abundance to your client base.
4. Note the results in your journal.

Part 9: The Close

> "A Champion never has the feeling they 'must close' every single deal.
>
> "The Champion is not afraid to 'lose' a prospect! They make a huge number of proposals to many prospects. They don't carefully choose the 'good' or 'happy' prospects. They don't spend a lot of time thinking or worrying, 'Should I tell this person about my products or not?' They just go ahead with no fear or worry, and confidently offer their product to a tremendous number of people."
> — Andrey Sizov

Advice #56
Don't Have a Scarcity Mindset

A Champion never has the feeling they "must close" every single deal.

The principle of a Champion is very simple: *The Champion invests themselves in everyone they meet, without "counting on" any one prospect. This is the key. They know they can change anyone's attitude positively, whether they close them or not.*

The Champion is not afraid to "lose" a prospect! They make a huge number of proposals to many prospects. They don't carefully choose the "good" or "happy" prospects. They don't spend a lot of time thinking or worrying, "Should I tell this person about my products or not?" They just go ahead with no fear or worry, and confidently offer their product to a tremendous number of people.

They never fear losing a specific prospect. They never allow themselves to get into a situation where they have a "shortage" of prospects. They always ensure they have an unlimited supply of prospects.

Andrey's Experience in London

Years ago in London I walked by a top-quality men's clothing store. Beautiful suits were displayed in the shop window. The prices were very high, even for London. The quality caught my attention and I stopped. The prices were way out of my league, but I was interested enough to walk in and take a closer look.

I was very alert and cautious. The salesman in the back of the store noticed me. He gave me time to look around and then greeted me: "Hello! I am here to help you, if you need me."

Afraid he would try to pressure me to buy something, I quickly told him, "I'm just looking."

He said, "I understand. Let's make a deal right now."

"What kind of deal? I am not buying anything!" I replied tensely.

He confidently stated, "That's fine. Let's make a deal that you are *not* buying anything from me now. You just look around. Let me explain why our shop is different from the others and why our prices are higher. We'll both agree you *can't buy* anything during this visit. If you decide to come back another time, I'll be more than glad to help you choose something you like. If you don't come back, that's okay, too. Deal?"

I agreed to that "deal" and I stayed. I relaxed. Here was a sales professional rich in prospects, totally confident of the quality and value of his products. He wasn't the owner, but he was proud of their high prices and he was not trying to talk me into buying anything. He didn't push me away. He treated me with respect and said "no" to me before I could say "no" to him.

The salesman toured me around the shop. He explained the purpose and philosophy of the owners, where the clothes came from and how they were made.

While I was listening to him, many things became clear to me. And the prices didn't seem as high as they did when I first walked in.

The salesman asked what I was interested in, and I said I

wanted to buy a beautiful tie that caught my eye as he was talking.

He said: "Great. It was a pleasure to talk with you. And now, have a nice evening."

"Wait a minute. I want to buy this tie."

He smiled and reminded me, "We made a deal when you walked in. You promised not to buy anything now."

I really wanted to buy that tie, so I said: "Nice joke. I'm serious, I really want to buy that tie."

He said calmly: "It wasn't a joke. I meant it. I didn't do this to trick you into buying something now. Many people leave and come back later to buy something."

I had to go out the front door, and then walk back in again to buy that tie, which I still own and use today!

Advice #57
Use "I'll Think About It" to Continue the Conversation

Did you ever find yourself, as a customer, in a situation where you didn't really see the benefit of something and didn't choose to buy, but you didn't want to upset the sales rep? So you ask, "Are you are open tomorrow? How late? Will you be here then? Great! I just need more time to think about it." Wasn't that an attempt to leave without making the sales rep upset?

This excuse can dispirit any sales rep. It decreases the willingness to continue and is often the reason why people don't want to work in sales! The sales rep believes that the customer really did go away to "think about" how they could buy it. But they normally never come back. Sound familiar to you?

Why does this happen? We want customers to buy now, not to "think about it and come back later." Understand this! They aren't going away to "think" — they're *just going away*.

Rule: *A sales rep should gradually, step by step, create the* **decision to act** *in the customer's mind.*

You can *use* any customer excuse:

- "I'll think about it."
- "We want to look at some other choices."
- "I need to talk to my spouse about it."
- "We will come back later this afternoon."

in order to *continue* to talk with the potential customer.

Their actual excuse can help you rekindle their interest in your product. Example: *"Yes, you should think about it. To make it easier for you, what is the benefit that you liked the most about this product? What problem are you trying to solve?"*

These and other similar questions give you the chance to find out what else they need to know about your product.

Use their excuse to ask more questions. Don't use pressure — just continue to be interested in their problems and invite them to talk about their issues. Don't just quit after you hear, "I'll think about it." Don't push, but also don't let go.

Nick's Experience: "Let Me Think About It"

I have a signature handling on the "let me think about it" objection, simply because salespeople hate it more than just about any other objection. But I actually found it the easiest of all objections to handle, and I've been using this handling successfully and teaching it for years.

The reason that "I'll think about it" is my signature objection handling is because a salesperson will do a fantastic presentation — the best they've ever done in their life. They get to the end and the prospect says, "I'll think about it" which can destroy an otherwise perfect presentation.

The whole idea of the handling is this: your prospect didn't wake up this morning and suddenly decide to purchase your product or service. They've most likely been thinking about it for some time.

If you look back at the Qualification section of this book,

and specifically advice #23, you dove in and got the prospect to tell you their real goals, problems and issues. As we advised back then, when your prospect reveals a goal, problem or issue, you must always ask them, "How long have you been thinking about that?"

It will normally have been quite a while. For a product or service in the utility industry, it's probably been years.

You'll discover that your prospect never even realizes how long they've been thinking about something like this until you ask the question. The purpose of asking the question is not just to get the answer, but to get the prospect to realize for *themselves* how long they've been thinking about it.

The answer from you, once they tell you how long they've been thinking about it, is always the same: "Wow! That's a long time!"

At that point, you've made it solid in their mind that they've been thinking about this problem, issue or goal for a substantial period of time.

Remember, this question is asked in the Qualify step. *Always* finish the Qualification step by asking: "How long have you been thinking about this?"

You make it through the rest of the sales process and you're ready for the Close.

If at that point they throw out, "I need to think about it," you're totally ready for them. You calmly say, "Sure, you could continue to think about it. But can I ask you a question? You told me earlier that you've been thinking about this for quite a long time. So, if I simply walk away and let you continue to think about it, that shows a genuine lack of caring on my part, doesn't it? Well, I'm just not willing to be that person."

Trust me, they won't have an answer for that — except to just sign up.

Quite frankly, since they already told you how long they've been "thinking about it" all the way back in the Qualify step, they actually know that it's a pretty weak objection if they raise it right at the close. So, 80 percent of the time they won't even bring it up.

Advice #58
Always Create Word of Mouth

Word of mouth has always existed, and it will always continue to exist. It is based on the natural willingness of people to share their feelings — good or bad. We are not talking about media advertising designed to make some product well known. We mean that people, as a rule, love to tell others about things they like or dislike. Their opinion about a product or service can often be the decisive factor for the people who trust them, their friends and family.

Rule: *Word of mouth is the best advertising.*

When your customer walks away with the *unshakable certainty* that their decision to buy from you was absolutely correct, you can be sure that you'll soon have several new customers referred to you.

By taking the time and care to create this unshakeable certainty about you and your product, you are creating your future income! *By selling with the future in mind, you make it possible for the customer to make their own decision based on certainty, which is the result of trust, security and lack of doubt.* The customer leaves knowing they can trust you, which means you must earn their trust in the beginning and maintain it throughout the sales process.

You should care about the customer, whether they buy something now or not. Tell them something interesting about your product. Find out what is important to them, and don't make a disgusted or disappointed face if they refuse to buy right now. You create trust with the customer by showing that you care more about their needs than your commission.

Show them the benefits of your knowledge, your product and your company, and you will create good will and a sense of trust. Do this, and then there is always the chance that either they themselves, their friends or their business partners will come back to you one more time. You will also feel better about yourself, your product and your company.

Continue to do this with every prospect, and you will create a future filled with high pay and people that trust you and refer their friends and family to you.

Jim's Story of the True Power of Word of Mouth

I was selling dry cleaning discount cards door-to-door early one Saturday, and the first house I came to belonged to an 87-year-old lady. I showed her the value of the discount cards and asked her about her family and friends.

After a few minutes I realized that she didn't qualify to buy the card, as she really didn't do enough dry cleaning. I thanked her, wished her a good day and turned to run to the next house.
To my surprise, she stopped me and said she wanted to buy one of the discount cards! I politely refused to sell her the card, because it would not benefit her, and I would feel bad about taking her money for nothing in exchange.

She insisted she wanted to buy one, and I realized she wanted to give me something just for being nice to her and listening to her stories of her grandchildren.

I asked if she had any chocolate chip cookies. She laughed and invited me in for cookies and milk.

I had already explained how the discount card worked, and she finally admitted she only took one blanket to be dry-cleaned every four years. Since there were 25 coupons on the card, this meant that the discount card would last her for another 100 years!

After a few minutes of friendly chatting and great cookies, I left, thanking her for the cookies and kindness.

As I approached the next house, the door opened before I could knock, and a young woman smiled and said, "Hello Jim! I'll take two please!"

I was shocked! I asked her what she was talking about. She said she had a check made out already for two dry-cleaning discount cards.

The nice little old lady next door was very well-known and loved in that neighborhood filled with young, urban, professional couples. She had called ahead and told everyone in the neighborhood that "Jim" was coming. She had memorized the sales pitch exactly and told each person that they should buy two. I made over $1,000 in commissions — a company sales record for a single day.

That is the power of word of mouth and an example of doing the right thing for the customer every time.

Energy Professionals Perspective

The backbone of prospecting can really be summed up in one word: *referrals*. In every industry and every business in the world, it is common knowledge that referrals — word of mouth — is the strongest, most stable and productive form of marketing. If you have many satisfied customers that share their positive experiences about you, your product or your service with other business owners, you quite literally have a marketing machine that will never stop bringing new customers.

But this also emphasizes one very, very important point: You must make sure your company can deliver what you promised would be delivered. In the commercial and industrial world, you, as the sales rep, are normally the most powerful voice for the customer.
Gone are the days when the sales division says "Quality Control" is not their responsibility. It ultimately is the energy consultant's responsibility to make sure the customer gets delivered what was promised. Any company that neglects their quality of delivery will not survive in the long run. Poor quality products or service creates word of mouth which spreads bad news like wildfire through the business community. So, don't fall into the trap of thinking that quality of product delivery is not your responsibility.

High-quality delivery is vital for creating referral sales. Even the best sales Champion in the world will fail if his company does not deliver what was promised.

You will find that people who are happy with the products and services are more than happy to give you plenty of referrals. Asking for referrals is one of the very important steps you can take to beat the "abundance versus scarcity" mindset. Getting referrals is also the real measure of a well-delivered sales experience and a true close.

"People influence people. Nothing influences people more than a recommendation from a trusted friend. A trusted referral influences people more than the best broadcast message. A trusted referral is the Holy Grail of advertising."
— Mark Zuckerberg

Action Items

1. Think of 5 happy customers, or prospects that had a positive experience with you in regard to your product or service.
2. Meet with them for the purpose of talking with them about the benefits that they've obtained from that product or service so far.
3. Talk with them until they become excited again about the product or service.
4. Ask for referrals and watch what happens. Decide to ask every customer you help for a referral.
5. Note the results in your journal.

Advice #59
Overcoming Your Worst Enemy: Doubt

Your worst enemy is the customer's *doubt* — not the price. There is a precise observation that proves that the more money someone pays, the more benefit they are able to get from any product or service.

Doubt, worry, uncertainty — they are the true enemies to every sales professional on the planet. And the weapon you use to handle it is *not* pressure or manipulation, but discussion of the *advantages* and *benefits* for the customer.

Don't use all your "bullets" at once. Use them one by one. You don't even know yet what exact "enemies" you will have to handle. You don't know, because in the beginning of the sale, you have neither doubt *nor* interest. Doubts will appear in the form of objections, then you will need your bullets — the benefits.

That's why you should start your pitch with the smaller advantages. Don't get yourself into the situation where the customer is almost ready to buy, and he gives you his last little doubt — which shows up in the form of an objection — and you have nothing left to say. Then you will feel pressure to make something up. This usually irritates them, and when they find out it's not true, it will destroy your future with this customer, as well as their friends and family.

Major error: Spill out all the benefits as fast as possible without keeping some as a reserve to handle any remaining objections (doubts).

Learn to engage your customer in a discussion of each

advantage or benefit of the product. Find out how it helps or handles a problem for them. Get them to participate in the conversation and tell you how this will profit their business or life.

Don't make the customer be a passive spectator of your "pitch." Customers will close *themselves* if you get them talking. Every good sales rep has heard this a million times, but it requires practice. Work on this skill every day, and both you and your customers will profit as a result.

And you will have a lot more fun every day!

Action Items

1. Review your product, service or company marketing materials. Figure out all of the advantages and benefits that you have to offer your customers.
2. List these points out, one by one.
3. Pick three of these points and figure out what "doubts" each would eliminate if they came up in conversation with your customer.
4. Note the results in your journal.

Advice #60
Learn from Your Mistakes and Move On — Mistakes Are Not Failures

People tend to get very upset when they fail.

Have you ever seen this happen? Has it ever happened to you? What is the best way to handle this?

We have observed a few ways that people tend to handle failure:

Never stick your neck out. Do nothing, then you can never fail.
They don't do anything because they are afraid to fail. Example: a sales rep doesn't walk up to a customer in the shop because they have learned that "customers hate to be hassled by sales reps." Sales reps tend to learn this lesson from a few disgruntled shoppers, then decide that the best thing to do is nothing. That store needs a good manager who can show the proper way to approach people actively but effectively. It's not very difficult to train anyone how to do this.

Be upset on the inside but pretend nothing has happened on the outside.
People who tend to do this build up internal pressure until they "crack" or "blow up."

The point of "blow up" is called "critical mass" in physics. Enough failures accumulate until (for no apparent reason) you see the explosion. If you look carefully, you can tell when a person is nearing *critical mass*: a strained smile, unnecessary chatter, fussiness, a sour look or sour words — "if you don't like it, don't buy it!" You probably remember times when you've seen these indicators around you, and you knew instinctively to get out of the way.

Then there is the best way. We call it *the principle of unsinkability*.
How does this work? Luckily, it's very simple.

What is failure? It's something people don't want to deal with. People don't like to see it, hear it, or talk about it. For example, when somebody refuses to take your call, it can make you feel like a failure.

Simply stated, a failure is anything that you don't want to be part of anymore.

Mistakes are not necessarily failures. If you learn from your mistakes, they become part of your education process, and you continue to move forward.

People who are actively trying to reach their goals make mistakes along the way. The trick is to learn from those mistakes and to continue to move toward your goal. Mistakes are part of living life.

But it's very easy to turn a mistake into a "failure." How? By refusing to look at the mistake because it's too painful or uncomfortable. Some people would rather pretend "everything's fine" or "nothing happened" or "it wasn't my fault." They are too worried about what others might think of them.

Those people who are actually busy doing something are making mistakes too, and they don't have time to laugh at your mistakes. In fact, they understand and will treat you respectfully, because they recognize that you are at least trying.

But if you insist on paying attention to the criticisms of the "unerring people" — the lazy cowards — you then start to back off from any mistake and avoid talking about it. As a result, there will be no lesson learned from it. Then you become more and more afraid of making mistakes. The more you fear something, the more you get what you fear. This is simple truth.

If you don't want "failure," then learn to communicate with your mistakes and be willing to learn from them.

In sales, most mistakes result in the customer refusing to buy from you. Embrace the "mistake." Review all of the steps of the sales process contained in this book, without blaming yourself or anyone else. You'll find that a failed sale probably had one of these steps undone or not completely done.

Find out how you could improve your handling of that customer and learn from this failed close. Do that, and you will never be a "failure."

Key principle of wealthy salespeople: *Communicate with each and every customer comfortably, confidently, never afraid of losing any customer, always willing to help a customer understand and let them walk away when necessary. Learn from your mistakes. UNSINKABILITY! This is one of the most important components of super successful sales reps!*

"The ambitious are criticized by those who have given up."
— Grant Cardone

Action Items

1. Review the 9 steps of the sales process used in this book.
2. List out 3 areas that you could improve in right away.
3. Note the results in your journal.
4. Be a prosperous, industrious sales Champion!

Be a Champion.

Find your passion. Tell others about your passion.

Practice, practice, practice!

Follow the advices and action items in this book.

You *can* be a wealthy sales Champion.

We wish you all the best!

Andrey & Jim

Rules, Laws and Principles

Sales is the service of helping a customer choose the best product or service.

— Advice #1

*To have more success and money in sales, be who you really are
and stop working under so much stress and strain.*

— Advice #3

Sell something you like, only take advice from a professional, ignore negative and critical people, and go into action.

— Advice #7

Love and pleasure from what you do directly influences your ability to have a lot of money without being stressed out.

— Advice #10

You should always be willing and able to just let the customer walk away.

— Advice #12

If you can't develop passion for your product and company, if you don't believe in the value of your product, you will tend to limit your own pay, whether you are aware of this principal or not. And you will tend to attract customer objections, even if they didn't have any objections in the first place.

In order to be a wealthy sales Champion, you have to sell a product you believe in and work for a company you can be proud of. It's your choice what you sell and who you work for. Choose wisely. Your success and happiness in this profession depend on your choice.

— Advice #14

Real success means willingness to talk to more and more people.

— Advice #15

*If you are willing to spend enough time and effective action
letting everyone know you have a good product, you will win.*

— Advice #20

You can always positively influence the customer's attitude.

— Advice #21

Be yourself! Learn to talk to people pleasantly, naturally, like you do with your friends, and then apply that same natural communication in sales. You and your customers will have more fun communicating with each other.

— Advice #28

The Champion always behaves the same way with the customer as they do in the rest of their life. They never have to pretend; they know what to say and do. And they learns this by practicing the art of sales every day.

— Advice #28

If you love what you are doing, you will be willing to complete a lot of actions every day. You will do these actions frequently, you will not stop doing these actions, you will be called "lucky" and you will make much more money easily.

— Advice #29

Help your customer by giving them the correct information to make the best choice and allowing them the right to not buy your product, and you won't become tired, you won't strain yourself, you will enjoy working with more people, and best of all, you won't be "fighting" your customers.

— Advice #31

The essence of your job is: To help the customer choose the best option for the customer!

— Advice #33

The customer buys the profit *not the* price!

Profit = Value minus Price. The profit is a positive difference between price and value; profit only becomes visible when the sales rep directs the customer's attention to the value — the price is normally obvious to the customer.

— Advice #34

Always love what you have and be willing to share with others. For a Champion it's a guiding rule. Champions focus on the positive in everything they do and have, and they are constantly trying to share this positive attitude with everyone they meet.

— Advice #39

Before you take, you must give.

— Advice 40

You either increase or decrease the value of your product in the customer's mind while you talk to them. The more you love your company and product, the more likely you are to increase the value and increase his willingness to deal with your company in the future.

— Advice #47

The real secret of product benefits is that the same benefit acts like a new and separate benefit every time it is brought to the customer's attention!

— Advice #49

Stop wasting your customer's time and attention by chattering nonsense, throwing worn out sales phrases and "closing" patter at them.

— Advice #53

A Sales rep should gradually, step by step, create the decision to act in the customer's mind.

— Advice #57

Word of mouth is the best advertising.

— Advice #58

Communicate with each and every customer comfortably, confidently, never afraid of losing any customer, always willing to help a customer understand and let them walk away when necessary. Learn from your mistakes. UNSINKABILITY! This is one of the most important components of super successful sales reps!

— Advice #60

A Code of Honor for Sales That Even an 8-Year-Old Would Understand

By Jim Mathers

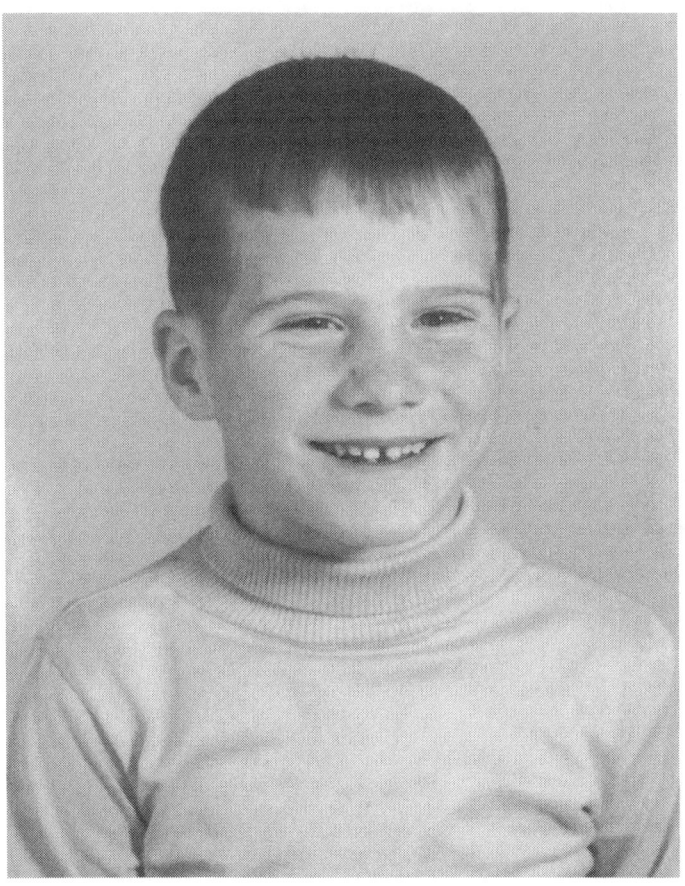

I was 8 years old in 1969.

I was told that if I wanted to go to Boy Scout summer camp in Northern Michigan, I would have to raise the $400 needed to pay for the camp and the transportation. My parents did not have enough money to pay for summer camp, neither did the other parents in our Detroit neighborhood. Times were tough in 1969. Money was tight. You wanted something extra, you found a way to pay for it yourself; one of my very first lessons as a junior entrepreneur.

Solution! The Boy Scout leadership in Michigan found a way to help the lower middle-class kids earn their way to camp. They were approached by Tom Wat enterprises. Tom Wat provided a large suitcase-like cardboard box filled with things like screw drivers, mini flashlights, and other handy dandy household items that everyone in the neighborhood would need.

I was so impressed! There were at least 25 useful items in the box, and everything sold for $10 each. I don't remember exactly how much Tom Wat kept, 50 to 75% I think, but each $10 sale put a couple dollars towards my Summer Camp expenses. I hit the streets immediately after I got my own parents to cough up $40 for several different "useful" tools. (They did not mind throwing in $40, since it saved them from finding $400 to make me happy.)

I was exhilarated! I was going to Summer Camp!

By the second weekend I was racking up the commissions and I was feeling confident of reaching my goal. I knew I was definitely going to make enough sales to got to Summer Camp.

Should be the end of the story right there. No big deal. Right?

Wrong.

The Boy Scout Oath of Honor: "On my honor, I will do my best, to do my duty, to God and my country, and to obey the Scout Law, to help other people at all times, to keep myself physically strong, mentally awake, and **morally straight**." (I added the emphasis to the last two words.)

In my mind, at 8 years of age, I took that Oath very seriously. I swore to uphold that Oath. I understood that morally straight meant being honest and doing the right thing for people. I really tried to be morally straight! Every day. I wasn't perfect. I have 2 sisters and 2 brothers and that alone is enough justification to knock you off the "morally straight" path occasionally.

Imagine how I felt when I found that the $10 "household items" were really 10 penny trinkets and only lasted a day or two before they broke and didn't work at all.

I knew one thing. I was not being morally straight. I violated my Oath. Yes... I was justified... I was doing the program that the Boy Scouts told us to do and the money was going to pay for summer camp.

My parents tried to console me. I tried to give them their money back. After all, my dad worked 70 hours a week to keep us fed and clothed and protected. I didn't want him to waste his money on objects that were worthless!

I collected thousands of dollars, $10 at a time, for worthless objects so I could go to Camp. Tom Wat made millions off the Boy Scouts. They took most of the money. Yes, they provided a game for young boys to create a business to make money for summer camp. Yes, I did go to summer camp because of Tom Wat. Yes, I mostly "forgot" about HOW I raised the money for summer camp.

Deep in my soul. I knew I broke that Oath of Honor. I knew that salesmen were terrible liars! Of course, because I was a "salesman" that summer and I was a terrible liar! I told my family and neighbors to buy these cool items for $10, and in exchange for a great household gadget, I was also going to raise enough money to go to summer camp.

I should have just asked each neighbor and family member to donate $10 to send me to camp. Their exchange would have been the satisfaction of helping a local boy spend the summer learning more about the Oath of Honor and Leadership and other valuable characteristics for a future citizen.

When I went to the US Naval Academy at Annapolis 10 years later (1979) I was a cocky varsity athlete, Honor Roll Academic and Student Council President. At the Naval Academy we took the Oath to protect and defend the Constitution of the United States.

Below is a comment on the Product of the US Naval Academy from a blog written by **Jacqui Murray** on March 26, 2010:

"The product of the Naval Academy is not an engineer, a political scientist, a chemist, or a physicist. The product is a citizen; a person formed in a heroic mold, who we hope will never have to be a hero, but who we are confident has the fortitude to go in harm's way to protect the Republic. The product is a person who will do the right thing for no other reason than it is the right thing to do. The product is a person who recognizes excellence and is willing to strive for it. The product is a person dedicated to caring for the enlisted men and women of the U.S. Navy, those people who do most of the work and most of the dying in our Navy."

I graduated from the Naval Academy in 1983. I knew one thing for sure. A small percentage of people did not follow the Code of Honor. But most of us did. I also knew another thing for sure. I was going to be a great engineer and help people after I got out of the US Navy in 1988. I had to serve my 5 years of active duty as a Submarine Officer first, but what was 5 years compared to the rest of my life? Being under water for 90 days at a time gave me lots of time to read and think about life.

So. What does the Naval Academy's Code of Honor and the Boy Scout Oath have to do with sales? What the heck does this story have to do with anything pertinent to life on this planet???

Deep down, I knew I had to be a good engineer to make a decent living in society, because... I sure was NOT going to be a salesman! I knew salesmen were liars and sold people things that broke and were useless. My experience as an 8-year old salesman set the tone for my life.

One big problem I ran into in 1988 when I got out of the Navy: engineers were not being paid very much. Booz Allen and Hamilton hired me for $35,000 a year. My rent was $18,000 a year. This was terrible. I was learning a financial lesson the hard way. After working for 20 years, the better engineers were making $70,000 a year. That was not good. How can you buy a decent house and drive a decent car and raise a few kids on $35-70,000 a year?

I knew a few salesmen who were making more money, but I also "knew" that I hated salesmen. Therefore, I could never be a salesman. Therefore, I was stuck making a limited income.

How do you re-define a concept that you had proved to be true beyond a shadow of a doubt when you were an 8-year old?

I wanted to make a lot more money than an engineer makes.

Luckily, I ran into a friend who was making $2,000 a week in door to door sales. He told me that I could double or triple my income if I learned how to sell. He also said that his product really helped people save money and it really worked. He explained the value and benefit of the product and it made sense to me, but I had this lingering feeling that he wasn't being honest with me.

Finally, he convinced me to go out and try to sell. I had nothing to lose except one Saturday of my life. I already gave the Navy 5 years of Saturdays, what was one more?

It was a simple discount card program for a local retailer. The company had been selling the same product in the same neighborhoods for 15 years. People loved this product and were happy to see the salesmen come back every year to renew the product.

I followed the expert around the block for an hour and watched him make sale after sale. No gimmicks. No lies. No double-talk. No BS. Just simple explanations, and he answered peoples' questions honestly.

I decided at that moment that not ALL salesmen are liars. Only the ones who knowingly sell a bad product or don't deliver the service they promised. I decided that I could sell and make a lot of money, but I would only sell products that I would willingly give to my own family and my 85-year-old grandmother. If the product or service was good enough for my family, then it would be good enough for the rest of the world.

That defining moment of my life was in the summer of 1989 in Washington DC. I've made millions of dollars in direct sales since that day. Not once have I sold a product or service that I was not proud to be associated with. I kept my word to myself. I kept my own Salesmen's Code of Honor the past 26 years.

Obviously, I no longer hate salesmen. I train salesmen to be professionals.

I respect sales professionals who follow the Code of Honor.

I wake up happy every day of the year because I'm surrounded by professionals who believe in the Code of Honor.

Take a look at your current product or service and be honest with yourself.

Good luck and have your best week ever!

Jim

Code of Honor for Millionaire Sales Professionals

1. Don't lie to the customer, ever.
2. Keep your promises to the customer, always.
3. If it is impossible to keep your promise, be forthright with the customer and tell them why you can't keep your promise and work out a solution that benefits the customer. Don't make the customer call you to complain. Call the customer first and present a solution.
4. Don't sell anything to the customer you would not want to buy yourself.
5. Don't do anything to the customer you would not want someone to do to you.
6. Treat the customer the way you want to be treated.
7. Don't lie to yourself, ever.
8. If you find out the product that you are selling is a rip off, and you would not give it to your own family for free, then have the guts to get out of that company and go find a product or service you can be proud to represent.
9. Learn everything you can about your product or service, so you can honestly answer the customer's questions.
10. Give the customer the right to walk away.
11. Be willing to walk away from the customer.
12. Don't get angry at the customer, it's inefficient and a waste of your time.
13. Don't degrade yourself, your product or your price. If you are selling a product or service that you are proud of, do not discount it.
14. It's okay to be a millionaire salesman. (Salesman = woman or man who is a professional in the honorable career of sales.)
15. If you want to be a millionaire salesman, follow this code of honor.

Summer of 1985:

Andrey was hunting American Nuclear Submarines as a Lieutenant on a Russian Anti-Submarine Corvette operating in the North Atlantic Ocean.

Jim was a Lieutenant aboard USS Flying Fish, SSN 683. The mission was to hunt down Russian Ballistic Missile Submarines operating in the North Atlantic Ocean.

In essence, Andrey was hunting Jim and Jim was hunting Andrey's friends (Russian Submarine Captains).

Map Image Credit: U.S. Geological Survey
Department of the Interior/USGS

Fall of 1985: Jim's submarine (USS Flying Fish, SSN 673) was operating in the Mediterranean Sea hunting Russian Ballistic Missile Submarines.

Map Image Credit: U.S. Geological Survey Department of the Interior/USGS

USS Flying Fish (SSN-673) at sea 1972
Jim Mathers served on the Flying Fish from May 1985 until May 1988.

Photo Credit: wikimedia.org Public Domain

It's cold up near the North Pole.

Courtesy of www.Hullnumber.com

Russian Anti Submarine Corvette Albatross Class
Lt. Andrey Sizov, Weapons Officer
http://www.zamotiviruy.ru/

Nanuchka Class Corvette similar to Andrey's corvette

Typical training exercise performed by Andrey's crew in the North Sea during the Cold War circa 1985.

Yes, that is frozen ice all over the ship. Russian sailors are tough! Obviously, Andrey had a much "colder" Cold War than Jim did inside his cozy submarine.

Jim with a couple of his classmates visiting the US Naval Academy in 1988.

From left to right: Marine Captain, Jeff Fletcher with his sons, Surface Warfare Officer, Lt. Sean "Sonny" O'Connor, and Submarine Warfare Officer, Lt. Jim Mathers.

All 3 were 1983 graduates of the US Naval Academy.

Jim in Moscow 2014

2013, Jim Mathers, Vlad Musatov, and Andrey Sizov. Jim and Andrey were guest speakers at Vlad's summer conference in St Petersburg, Russia.

Andrey delivering motivational seminar in Kiev, 2015

Andrey in Kiev, 2015

Andrey: having fun in Kiev, 2015

Jim with Grant and Elena Cardone in Moscow, 2014. Jim and Grant addressed nearly 1,000 Russian business owners and managers on sales and marketing secrets.

Moscow, 2014: Listening to Grant Cardone enlighten and entertain at the same time

Andrey & Jim with Grant & Elena speaking to Russian business leaders in Moscow 2014

Jim was guest speaker in St Petersburg, Russia, 2014

St Petersburg Russia, 2015: Jim's translator, Tanya Markova

Jim in Moscow's Red Square, 2014

Jim & Andrey in Moscow, 2014

Jim & Andrey, St Petersburg, 2012

Jim & Fu Mei Mathers with Andrey and Elena Sizov, St Petersburg, 2012

Leadership Award, 2012

Jim in Taipei, Taiwan; Moonlight Sales Seminar, 2012

Jim & Andrey in St Petersburg, 2013

Moscow awards ceremony 2012

After seminar in Riga, Latvia, 2012

Jim delivering seminars in Brazil, 2016

Happy readers with their Portuguese copy of Ending the War Between Salesmen & Customers

Jim delivering Seminars in Tolyatti, Russia 2016

Jim delivering seminars in Kazakhstan, 2016

Jim with business seminar organizer in Odessa, Ukraine 2016

Jim giving sales training to his friends in St Petersburg, Russia, 2014

We want you to succeed beyond your wildest dreams!!!!

The reason we included all these photos of our friends around the world is to point out one important thing. These people are people. They are hard working men and women.

If we take language out of the equation, we could be friends very easily. Which proves that with effective communication, any problem can be solved without fighting.

Yes! We are optimistic about the future. And we wish to share that optimism with our friends on all continents, not just Russia and the USA.

We hope to see you soon!

Jim & Andrey

Made in the USA
Las Vegas, NV
25 November 2024